W9-AAP-833

Sociology

By George D. Zgourides, Psy. D., and
Christie S. Zgourides, M.A.

IDG Books Worldwide, Inc.
An International Data Group Company
Foster City, CA ♦ Chicago, IL ♦ Indianapolis, IN ♦ New York, NY

About the Author

George Zgourides, Psy.D., is a licensed clinical psychologist specializing in anxiety, phobias, sexuality, Traditional Chinese Medicine (TCM) approaches to healing, and the sociology of religion. His academic appointments have included Assistant Professor of Psychology at the University of Portland (Portland, Oregon), Associate Professor of Psychology and Sociology at New Mexico Military Institute (Roswell, New Mexico), and Academic Dean at the Dallas Institute of Acupuncture and Oriental Medicine (Dallas, Texas).

Publisher's Acknowledgments

Editorial

Project Editor: Kathleen M. Cox

Acquisitions Editor: Kris Fulkerson

Copy Editor: Corey Dalton

Editorial Assistant: Carol Strickland

Production

Proofreader: Jeannie Smith

IDG Books Indianapolis Production Department

CLIFFSQUICKREVIEW™ Sociology

Published by

IDG Books Worldwide, Inc.

An International Data Group Company

919 E. Hillsdale Blvd.

Suite 400

Foster City, CA 94404

www.idgbooks.com (IDG Books Worldwide Web site)

www.cliffsnotes.com (CliffsNotes Web site)

Library of Congress Control Number: 00-104212

ISBN: 0-7645-8615-7

Printed in the United States of America

10 9 8 7 6 5 4 3 2 1

1O/RS/QX/QQ/IN

Distributed in the United States by IDG Books Worldwide, Inc.

Distributed by CDG Books Canada Inc. for Canada; by Transworld Publishers Limited in the United Kingdom; by IDG Norge Books for Norway; by IDG Sweden Books for Sweden; by IDG Books Australia Publishing Corporation Pty. Ltd. for Australia and New Zealand; by TransQuest Publishers Pte Ltd. for Singapore, Malaysia, Thailand, Indonesia, and Hong Kong; by Gotop Information Inc. for Taiwan; by ICG Muse, Inc. for Japan; by Intersoft for South Africa; by Eyrolles for France; by International Thomson Publishing for Germany, Austria and Switzerland; by Distribuidora Cuspide for Argentina; by LR International for Brazil; by Galileo Libros for Chile; by Ediciones ZETA S.C.R. Ltda. for Peru; by WS Computer Publishing Corporation, Inc., for the Philippines; by Contemporanea de Ediciones for Venezuela; by Express Computer Distributors for the Caribbean and West Indies; by Micronesia Media Distributor, Inc. for Micronesia; by Chips Computadoras S.A. de C.V. for Mexico; by Editorial Norma de Panama S.A. for Panama; by American Bookshops for Finland.

For general information on IDG Books Worldwide's books in the U.S., please call our Consumer Customer Service department at **800-762-2974.** For reseller information, including discounts and premium sales, please call our Reseller Customer Service department at **800-434-3422.**

For information on where to purchase IDG Books Worldwide's books outside the U.S., please contact our International Sales department at **317-596-5530** or fax **317-572-4002.**

For consumer information on foreign language translations, please contact our Customer Service department at **1-800-434-3422,** fax 317-572-4002, or e-mail rights@idgbooks.com.

For information on licensing foreign or domestic rights, please phone **650-653-7098**.

For sales inquiries and special prices for bulk quantities, please contact our Order Services department at **800-434-3422** or write to the address above.

For information on using IDG Books Worldwide's books in the classroom or for ordering examination copies, please contact our Educational Sales department at **800-434-2086** or fax **317-572-4005.**

For press review copies, author interviews, or other publicity information, please contact our Public Relations department at **650-653-7000** or fax **650-653-7500.**

For authorization to photocopy items for corporate, personal, or educational use, please contact Copyright Clearance Center, 222 Rosewood Drive, Danvers, MA 01923, or fax **978-750-4470.**

CONTENTS

CONTENTS

CONTENTS

CONTENTS

CONTENTS

CONTENTS

CONTENTS

CONTENTS

CONTENTS

Sociology is the scientific study of human groups and social behavior. Sociologists focus primarily on human interactions, including how social relationships influence people's attitudes and how societies form and change. Sociology, therefore, is a discipline of broad scope: Virtually no topic—gender, race, religion, politics, education, health care, drug abuse, pornography, group behavior, conformity—is taboo for sociological examination and interpretation.

Sociological Imagination

Sociologists typically focus their studies on how people and society influence other people, because external, or social, forces shape most personal experiences. These social forces exist in the form of interpersonal relationships among family and friends, as well as among the people encountered in academic, religious, political, economic, and other types of social institutions. In 1959, sociologist C. Wright Mills defined **sociological imagination** as the ability to see the impact of social forces on individuals' private and public lives. Sociological imagination, then, plays a central role in the sociological perspective.

As an example, consider a depressed individual. You may reasonably assume that a person becomes depressed when something "bad" has happened in his or her life. But you cannot so easily explain depression in all cases. How do you account for depressed people who have not experienced an unpleasant or negative event?

Sociologists look at events from a **holistic**, or multidimensional, perspective. Using sociological imagination, they examine both personal and social forces when explaining any phenomenon. Another version of this holistic model is the **biopsychosocial** perspective, which attributes complex sociological phenomena to interacting biological (internal), psychological (internal), and social (external) forces. In the case of depression, chemical imbalances in the brain (biological), negative attitudes (psychological), and an impoverished home environment (social) can all contribute to the problem. The **reductionist** perspective, which "reduces" complex sociological phenomena to a single "simple" cause, stands in contrast to the holistic perspective. A reductionist may claim that you can treat all cases of depression with medication because all depression comes from chemical imbalances in the brain.

On a topic related to depression, French sociologist Emile Durkheim studied suicide in the late 19th century. Being interested in the differences in rates of suicide across assorted peoples and countries and groups, Durkheim found that social rather than personal influences primarily caused these rates. To explain these differences in rates of suicide, Durkheim examined **social integration**, or the degree to which people connect to a social group. Interestingly, he found that when social integration is either deficient or excessive, suicide rates tend to be higher. For example, he found that divorced people are more likely to experience poor social integration, and thus are more likely to commit suicide than are married people. As another example, in the past, Hindu widows traditionally committed ritualistic suicide (called "suttee" meaning "good women") because the cultural pressure at the time to kill themselves overwhelmed them.

Social forces are powerful, and social groups are more than simply the sum of their parts. Social groups have characteristics that come about only when individuals interact. So the sociological perspective and the social imagination help sociologists to explain these social forces and characteristics, as well as to apply their findings to everyday life.

Sociology and Common Sense

Many people mistakenly believe that sociology is the study of the obvious. They claim that sociology is nothing but the application of common sense. But equating any science with simple common sense could not be further from the truth! Common sense is not always "common," nor "sensible." Statements like "Birds of a feather flock together" and "Opposites attract," while supposedly based on common knowledge, contradict each other. Because common sense does not always accurately predict reality, people need something else.

Not every sociological finding is revolutionary; many findings do appear consistent with common sense. By systematically testing common sense beliefs against facts, sociologists can sort out which popular beliefs hold true and which do not. To accomplish this, sociologists use a variety of social science research designs and methods. (See Chapter 2 for more on the scientific basis of sociology.)

Sociology as a discipline is more than common sense. Sociology is a method of inquiry that requires the systematic testing of beliefs against evidence. Sociologists, therefore, make determining whether specific ideas are fact or fiction their job.

The Founders of Sociology

Each field of academic study has its own cast of characters, and sociology is no exception. Although countless individuals have contributed to sociology's development into a social science, several individuals deserve special mention.

Auguste Comte

The French philosopher **Auguste Comte** (1798–1857)—often called the "father of sociology"—first used the term "sociology" in 1838 to refer to the scientific study of society. He believed that all societies develop and progress through the following stages: religious, metaphysical, and scientific. Comte argued that society needs scientific knowledge based on facts and evidence to solve its problems—not speculation and superstition, which characterize the religious and metaphysical stages of social development. Comte viewed the science of sociology as consisting of two branches: **dynamics**, or the study of the processes by which societies change; and **statics**, or the study of the processes by which societies endure. He also envisioned sociologists as eventually developing a base of scientific social knowledge that would guide society into positive directions.

Herbert Spencer

The 19th-century Englishman **Herbert Spencer** (1820–1903) compared society to a living organism with interdependent parts. Change in one part of society causes change in the other parts, so that every part contributes to the stability and survival of society as a whole. If one part of society malfunctions, the other parts must adjust to the crisis and contribute even more to preserve society. Family, education, government, industry, and religion comprise just a few of the parts of the "organism" of society.

Spencer suggested that society will correct its own defects through the natural process of "survival of the fittest." The societal "organism" naturally leans toward homeostasis, or balance and stability. Social problems work themselves out when the government leaves society alone. The "fittest"—the rich, powerful, and successful—enjoy their status because nature has "selected" them to do so. In contrast, nature has doomed the "unfit"—the poor, weak, and unsuccessful—to failure. They must fend for themselves without social assistance if society is to remain healthy and even progress to higher levels. Governmental interference in the "natural" order of society weakens society by wasting the efforts of its leadership in trying to defy the laws of nature.

Karl Marx

Not everyone has shared Spencer's vision of societal harmony and stability. Chief among those who disagreed was the German political philosopher and economist **Karl Marx** (1818–1883), who observed society's exploitation of the poor by the rich and powerful. Marx argued that Spencer's healthy societal "organism" was a falsehood. Rather than interdependence and stability, Marx claimed that social conflict, especially class conflict, and competition mark all societies.

The class of capitalists that Marx called the **bourgeoisie** particularly enraged him. Members of the bourgeoisie own the means of production and exploit the class of laborers, called the **proletariat**, who do not own the means of production. Marx believed that the very natures of the bourgeoisie and the proletariat inescapably lock the two classes in conflict. But he then took his ideas of class conflict one step further: He predicted that the laborers are not selectively "unfit," but are destined to overthrow the capitalists. Such a class revolution would establish a "class-free" society in which all people work according to their abilities and receive according to their needs.

Unlike Spencer, Marx believed that economics, not natural selection, determines the differences between the bourgeoisie and the proletariat. He further claimed that a society's economic system decides peoples' norms, values, mores, and religious beliefs, as well as the nature of the society's political, governmental, and educational systems. Also unlike Spencer, Marx urged people to take an active role in changing society rather than simply trusting it to evolve positively on its own.

Emile Durkheim

Despite their differences, Marx, Spencer, and Comte all acknowledged the importance of using science to study society, although none actually used scientific methods. Not until **Emile Durkheim** (1858–1917) did a person systematically apply scientific methods to sociology as a discipline. A French philosopher and sociologist, Durkheim stressed the importance of studying **social facts**, or patterns of behavior characteristic of a particular group. The phenomenon of suicide especially interested Durkheim (as noted in the section "Sociological Imagination," earlier in this chapter). But he did not limit his ideas on the topic to mere speculation. Durkheim formulated his conclusions about the causes of suicide based on the analysis of large amounts of statistical data collected from various European countries.

Durkheim certainly advocated the use of systematic observation to study sociological events, but he also recommended that sociologists avoid considering people's attitudes when explaining society. Sociologists should only consider as objective "evidence" what they themselves can directly observe. In other words, they must not concern themselves with people's subjective experiences.

Max Weber

The German sociologist **Max Weber** (1864–1920) disagreed with the "objective evidence only" position of Durkheim. He argued that sociologists must also consider people's interpretations of events—not just the events themselves. Weber believed that individuals' behaviors cannot exist apart from their interpretations of the meaning of their own behaviors, and that people tend to act according to these interpretations. Because of the ties between objective behavior and subjective interpretation, Weber believed that sociologists must inquire into people's thoughts, feelings, and perceptions regarding their own behaviors. Weber recommended that sociologists adopt his method of *Verstehen* (vûrst e hen), or empathetic understanding. Verstehen allows sociologists to mentally put themselves into "the other person's shoes" and thus obtain an "interpretive understanding" of the meanings of individuals' behaviors.

Sociology in America

Sociology made its way from Europe to the United States by the turn of the 20th century. Like their European predecessors and counterparts, early American sociologists attempted to understand and solve the problems of their day, including crime, racial problems, and economic woes. But unlike the Europeans, who were more interested in forming large-scale social theories, American sociologists tried to develop pragmatic solutions to specific problems, such as child labor.

Jane Addams and Hull House

Jane Addams (1860–1935) was a preeminent founder of American sociology. She set up her Chicago-based "Hull House" as a center for sociological research. Most of the sociologists at Hull House were women who enjoyed applying sociological knowledge to solve social problems such as unfair labor policies, exploitation of children and workers, poverty, juvenile delinquency, and discrimination against women, minorities, and the elderly. These sociologists also used a research technique known as **mapping**, in which they collected **demographic data** such as age, gender, and socioeconomic status, geographically distributed this information, and then analyzed the distribution. After identifying problems and devising a social-action policy based on available data, they would organize community members and lobby political leaders to solve the problem. Addams, who won the Nobel Peace Prize in 1931, played a major part in establishing government safety and health standards and regulations, as well as founding important government programs, including Social Security, Workers' Compensation, and the Children's Bureau.

Both an applied and a basic science

For about the first 40 years of the 20th century, most American sociologists emphasized the practical aspects of the field, especially in terms of initiating various social reforms. That is, they viewed sociology as an **applied** social science (applying their knowledge to create practical solutions to societal problems). Later, when sociologists became more interested in developing general theories of how society works, many viewed sociology as a **basic** social science, (seeking knowledge for the sake of knowledge only). Along with the ideal of knowledge for its own sake came the notion that sociology should be "pure" and objective—without values, opinions, or agendas for social reform. As a result, between 1940 and 1960, sociologists developed and applied rigorous and sophisticated scientific methods to the study of social behavior and societies.

In the 1960s, however, people began to challenge sociology's objective and value-free approach to social knowledge. An increased awareness of and interest in such social ills as racial unrest, gender inequity, poverty, and controversy over the Vietnam War led society once again to look for the practical solutions associated with sociology as an applied science.

At the dawn of the 21st century, sociology in America is a social science that is both applied and basic, subjective and objective. In addition, the discipline has divided into many specialties and subspecialties—from **industrial sociology** (the application of sociological principles to solving industrial and business problems) to **ethnomethodology** (the scientific study of common sense) to **clinical sociology** (the application of sociological principles to solving human problems and effecting social change). Today, the number of sociologists stands at about 20,000.

Three Major Perspectives in Sociology

Sociologists analyze social phenomena at different levels and from different perspectives. From concrete interpretations to sweeping generalizations of society and social behavior, sociologists study everything from specific events (the **micro** level of analysis of small social patterns) to the "big picture" (the **macro** level of analysis of large social patterns).

The pioneering European sociologists, however, also offered a broad conceptualization of the fundamentals of society and its workings. Their views form the basis for today's theoretical perspectives, or **paradigms**, which provide sociologists with an orienting framework—a philosophical position—for asking certain kinds of questions about society and its people.

Sociologists today employ three primary theoretical perspectives: the symbolic interactionist perspective, the functionalist perspective, and the conflict perspective. These perspectives offer sociologists theoretical paradigms for explaining how society influences people, and vice versa. Each perspective uniquely conceptualizes society, social forces, and human behavior (see Table 1-1).

Table 1-1: Sociological Perspectives

Sociological Perspective	Level of Analysis	Focus
1. Symbolic Interactionism	Micro	Use of symbols Face-to-face interactions
2. Functionalism	Macro	Relationship between the parts of society How aspects of society are functional (adaptive)
3. Conflict Theory	Macro	Competition for scarce resources How the elite control the poor and weak

The symbolic interactionist perspective

The **symbolic interactionist perspective**, also known as **symbolic interactionism**, directs sociologists to consider the symbols and details of everyday life, what these symbols mean, and how people interact with each other. Although symbolic interactionism traces its origins to Max Weber's assertion that individuals act according to their interpretation of the meaning of their world, the American philosopher **George H. Mead** (1863–1931) introduced this perspective to American sociology in the 1920s.

According to the symbolic interactionist perspective, people attach meanings to symbols, and then they act according to their subjective interpretation of these symbols. Verbal conversations, in which spoken words serve as the predominant symbols, make this subjective interpretation especially evident. The words have a certain meaning for the "sender," and, during effective communication, they hopefully have the same meaning for the "receiver." In other terms, words are not static "things"; they require intention and interpretation. Conversation is an interaction of symbols between individuals who constantly interpret the world around them. Of course, anything can serve as a symbol as long as it refers to something beyond itself. Written music serves as an example. The black dots and lines become more than mere marks on the page; they refer to notes organized in such a way as to make musical sense. Thus, symbolic interactionists give serious thought to how people act, and then seek to determine what meanings individuals assign to their own actions and symbols, as well as to those of others.

Consider applying symbolic interactionism to the American institution of marriage. Symbols may include wedding bands, vows of lifelong commitment, a white bridal dress, a wedding cake, a Church ceremony, and flowers and music. American society attaches general meanings to these symbols, but individuals also maintain their own perceptions of what these and other symbols mean. For example, one of the spouses may see their circular wedding rings as symbolizing "never ending love," while the other may see them as a mere financial expense. Much faulty communication can result from differences in the perception of the same events and symbols.

Critics claim that symbolic interactionism neglects the macro level of social interpretation—the "big picture." In other words, symbolic interactionists may miss the larger issues of society by focusing too closely on the "trees" (for example, the size of the diamond in the wedding ring) rather than the "forest" (for example, the quality of the marriage). The perspective also receives criticism for slighting the influence of social forces and institutions on individual interactions.

The functionalist perspective

According to the **functionalist perspective**, also called **functionalism**, each aspect of society is interdependent and contributes to society's functioning as a whole. The government, or state, provides education for the children of the family, which in turn pays taxes on which the state depends to keep itself running. That is, the family is dependent upon the school to help children grow up to have good jobs so that they can raise and support their own families. In the process, the children become law-abiding, taxpaying citizens, who in turn support the state. If all goes well, the parts of society produce order, stability, and productivity. If all does not go well, the parts of society then must adapt to recapture a new order, stability, and productivity. For example, during a financial recession with its high rates of unemployment and inflation, social programs are trimmed or cut. Schools offer fewer programs. Families tighten their budgets. And a new social order, stability, and productivity occur.

Functionalists believe that society is held together by **social consensus**, or cohesion, in which members of the society agree upon, and work together to achieve, what is best for society as a whole. Emile Durkheim suggested that social consensus takes one of two forms:

- **Mechanical solidarity** is a form of social cohesion that arises when people in a society maintain similar values and beliefs and engage in similar types of work. Mechanical solidarity most commonly occurs in traditional, simple societies such as those in which everyone herds cattle or farms. Amish society exemplifies mechanical solidarity.

- In contrast, **organic solidarity** is a form of social cohesion that arises when the people in a society are interdependent, but hold to varying values and beliefs and engage in varying types of work. Organic solidarity most commonly occurs in industrialized, complex societies such those in large American cities like New York in the 2000s.

The functionalist perspective achieved its greatest popularity among American sociologists in the 1940s and 1950s. While European functionalists originally focused on explaining the inner workings of social order, American functionalists focused on discovering the functions of human behavior. Among these American functionalist sociologists is **Robert Merton** (b. 1910), who divides human functions into two types: **manifest functions** are intentional and obvious, while **latent functions** are unintentional and not obvious. The manifest function of attending a church or synagogue, for instance, is to worship as part of a religious community, but its latent function may be to help members learn to discern personal from institutional values. With common sense, manifest functions become easily apparent. Yet this is not necessarily the case for latent functions, which often demand a sociological approach to be revealed. A sociological approach in functionalism is the consideration of the relationship between the functions of smaller parts and the functions of the whole.

Functionalism has received criticism for neglecting the negative functions of an event such as divorce. Critics also claim that the perspective justifies the status quo and complacency on the part of society's members. Functionalism does not encourage people to take an active role in changing their social environment, even when such change may benefit them. Instead, functionalism sees active social change as undesirable because the various parts of society will compensate naturally for any problems that may arise.

The conflict perspective

The conflict perspective, which originated primarily out of Karl Marx's writings on class struggles, presents society in a different light than do the functionalist and symbolic interactionist perspectives. While these latter perspectives focus on the positive aspects of society that contribute to its stability, the **conflict perspective** focuses on the negative, conflicted, and ever-changing nature of society. Unlike functionalists who defend the status quo, avoid social change, and believe people cooperate to effect social order, conflict theorists challenge the status quo, encourage social change (even when this means social revolution), and believe rich and powerful people force social order on the poor and the weak. Conflict theorists, for example, may interpret an "elite" board of regents raising tuition to pay for esoteric new programs that raise the prestige of a local college as self-serving rather than as beneficial for students.

Whereas American sociologists in the 1940s and 1950s generally ignored the conflict perspective in favor of the functionalist, the tumultuous 1960s saw American sociologists gain considerable interest in conflict theory. They also expanded Marx's idea that the key conflict in society was strictly economic. Today, conflict theorists find social conflict between any groups in which the potential for inequality exists: racial, gender, religious, political, economic, and so on. Conflict theorists note that unequal groups usually have conflicting values and agendas, causing them to compete against one another. This constant competition between groups forms the basis for the ever-changing nature of society.

Critics of the conflict perspective point to its overly negative view of society. The theory ultimately attributes humanitarian efforts, altruism, democracy, civil rights, and other positive aspects of society to capitalistic designs to control the masses, not to inherent interests in preserving society and social order.

Other Perspectives

In addition to the three theoretical paradigms previously presented, sociologists use many different models to examine, describe, and understand society and human behavior. Some of the more popular, which are normally used as adjuncts to the above paradigms, include the cross-species perspective, cross-cultural perspective, statistical perspective, historical perspective, religious perspective, and feminist perspective. Each of these is limited in its ability to comprehensively describe society and behavior. Instead, they complement the other, larger, paradigms.

The cross-species perspective

Obviously, human beings belong to the animal kingdom. The **cross-species perspective** considers the similarities in and differences between human social behavior and that of other animals. A comparison of social behaviors across species can provide valuable insights into the nature of human society.

The cross-cultural perspective

The study of sociology must address cultural differences and issues. Research studies and social investigations have determined that beliefs, practices, and values certainly differ considerably from culture to culture. That which is acceptable to one group may not be to another. Hence, the **cross-cultural perspective** deals with the comparative nature of customs and standards of behavior within a community or system.

Remaining alert to cultural differences increases opportunities to challenge **gender-role stereotypes**, or beliefs within a society as to how members of each sex should appear and act. The cross-cultural perspective, then, takes into account the many variations that exist across societies and cultures.

The statistical perspective

The **statistical perspective** is based on the frequency of occurrence of an attitude or practice within a society. Although extremes occur within any group, statistical measurement is concerned with the characteristics of the largest number of members of a society—that is, the average members' characteristics.

The historical perspective

The **historical perspective** deals with social issues from the point of view of historical attitudes, values, practices, and contexts. Making sense of the many complex issues associated with society is easier when one examines the roles that such issues have played in history.

The religious perspective

The **religious perspective** considers the effects that religious doctrines, scriptures, and spirituality have on individuals and society. For people raised in a religious environment, the teachings, morals, and values set forth by organized religion can play a powerful role for life, be it healthy, harmful, or neutral.

The feminist perspective

The **feminist perspective** is concerned with gender differences and the limitations associated with traditional, male-dominated theories of society. Feminists also claim that their insights provide additional information about the experiences of both males and females. The perspective has received criticism for overstating the influence and prevalence of male power and control over women. Critics point out that many men only appear to have power and control over women.

An Integrated Perspective

Taken alone, any of the perspectives noted in this chapter may present a single-sided, distorted picture of society and human behavior. Although each provides a unique framework for studying society, none is complete by itself. The world is too complex to rely on reductionistic approaches or to "take it all in at once." Each sociological perspective clarifies some aspect of society and human behavior. Sometimes these perspectives complement each other, and sometimes they contradict each other. When integrated, however, these perspectives give sociologists the opportunity to gain the fullest possible sociological understanding.

The definition of sociology given in Chapter 1 uses the phrase "scientific study." Many people do not consider the social or *soft* sciences—such as sociology and psychology—to be "true" or *hard* sciences—such as chemistry and physics.

Whereas inherent differences exist between the soft and hard sciences, the same fundamental principles of scientific inquiry apply. The word *science* comes from the Latin *scire* meaning "to know," and for centuries "science" referred to virtually any academic discipline, including theology, languages, and literature. Only in the last hundred years or so has *science* come to mean a field of study that relies on specific research values and methods. (Remember that Emile Durkheim in the late 19th century was the first sociologist to use the scientific method.) Thus, whether or not a particular discipline like sociology is a science depends more on the methods used than on the particular subject area studied.

Scientific Method

An area of inquiry is a **scientific discipline** if its investigators use the **scientific method**, which is a systematic approach to researching questions and problems through objective and accurate **observation**, **collection and analysis of data**, **direct experimentation**, and **replication** (repeating) of these procedures. Scientists affirm the importance of gathering information carefully, remaining unbiased when evaluating information, observing phenomena, conducting experiments, and accurately recording procedures and results. They are also skeptical about their results, so they repeat their work and have their findings confirmed by other scientists.

Is sociological research scientific? Yes! By definition, **sociological research** is the scientific means of acquiring information about various aspects of society and social behavior. Sociologists use the scientific method. Like other scientists, they stress the accurate and unbiased collection and analysis of social data, use systematic observation, conduct experiments, and exhibit skepticism.

Basic Concepts in Social Science Research

An investigator begins a research study after evolving ideas from a specific **theory**, which is an integrated set of statements for explaining various phenomena. Because a theory is too general to test, the investigator devises a **hypothesis**, or testable prediction, from the theory, and tests this instead. The results of the research study either disprove or do not disprove the hypothesis. If disproved, the investigator cannot make predictions based on the hypothesis, and must question the accuracy of the theory. If not disproved, the scientist can make predictions based on the hypothesis.

A goal of sociological research is to discover the similarities, differences, patterns, and trends of a given **population**. Members of a population who participate in a study are **subjects** or **respondents**. When the characteristics of a **sample** of the population are representative of the characteristics of the entire population, scientists can apply, or **generalize**, their findings to the entire population. The best and most representative sample is a **random sample**, in which each member of a population has an equal chance of being chosen as a subject.

In **quantitative research**, information collected from respondents (for example, a respondent's college ranking) is converted into numbers (for example, a junior may equal three and a senior four). In **qualitative research**, information collected from respondents takes the form of verbal descriptions or direct observations of events. Although verbal descriptions and observations are useful, many scientists prefer quantitative data for purposes of analysis.

To analyze data, scientists use **statistics**, which is a collection of mathematical procedures for describing and drawing inferences from the data. Two types of statistics are most common: **inferential**, used for making predictions about the population, and **descriptive**, used for describing the characteristics of the population and respondents. Scientists use both types of statistics to draw general conclusions about the population being studied and the sample.

A scientist who uses a questionnaire or test in a study is interested in the test's **validity**, which is its capacity to measure what it purports to measure. He or she is also interested in its **reliability**, or capacity to provide consistent results when administered on different occasions.

Research Designs and Methods in Sociology

Sociologists use many different designs and methods to study society and social behavior. Most sociological research involves **ethnography**, or "field work" designed to depict the characteristics of a population as fully as possible.

Three popular social research **designs** (models) are

- **Cross-sectional**, in which scientists study a number of individuals of different ages who have the same trait or characteristic of interest at a single time

- **Longitudinal**, in which scientists study the same individuals or society repeatedly over a specified period of time

- **Cross-sequential**, in which scientists test individuals in a cross-sectional sample more than once over a specified period of time

Six of the most popular sociological research **methods** (procedures) are the *case study, survey, observational, correlational,* *experimental,* and *cross-cultural* methods, as well as working with information already available.

Case study research

In **case study research**, an investigator studies an individual or small group of individuals with an unusual condition or situation. Case studies are typically clinical in scope. The investigator (often a clinical sociologist) sometimes uses self-report measures to acquire quantifiable data on the subject. A comprehensive case study, including a long-term follow-up, can last months or years.

On the positive side, case studies obtain useful information about individuals and small groups. On the negative side, they tend to apply only to individuals with similar characteristics rather than to the general population. The high likelihood of the investigator's biases affecting subjects' responses limits the generalizability of this method.

Survey research

Survey research involves interviewing or administering **questionnaires**, or written surveys, to large numbers of people. The investigator analyzes the data obtained from surveys to learn about similarities, differences, and trends. He or she then makes predictions about the population being studied.

As with most research methods, survey research brings both advantages and disadvantages. Advantages include obtaining information from a large number of respondents, conducting personal interviews at a time convenient for respondents, and acquiring data as inexpensively as possible. "Mail-in" surveys have the added advantage of ensuring anonymity and thus prompting respondents to answer questions truthfully.

Disadvantages of survey research include **volunteer bias**, **interviewer bias**, and **distortion**. **Volunteer bias** occurs when a sample of volunteers is not representative of the general population. Subjects who are willing to talk about certain topics may answer surveys differently than those who are not willing to talk. **Interviewer bias** occurs when an interviewer's expectations or insignificant gestures (for example, frowning or smiling) inadvertently influence a subject's responses one way or the other. **Distortion** occurs when a subject does not respond to questions honestly.

Observational research

Because distortion can be a serious limitation of surveys, **observational research** involves directly observing subjects' reactions, either in a laboratory (called **laboratory observation**) or in a natural setting (called **naturalistic observation**). Observational research reduces the possibility that subjects will not give totally honest accounts of the experiences, not take the study seriously, fail to remember, or feel embarrassed.

Observational research has limitations, however. Subject bias is common, because volunteer subjects may not be representative of the general public. Individuals who agree to observation and monitoring may function differently than those who do not. They may also function differently in a laboratory setting than they do in other settings.

Correlational research

A sociologist may also conduct **correlational research**. A **correlation** is a relationship between two **variables** (or "factors that change"). These factors can be characteristics, attitudes, behaviors, or events. Correlational research attempts to determine if a relationship exists between the two variables, and the degree of that relationship.

A social researcher can use case studies, surveys, interviews, and observational research to discover correlations. Correlations are either positive (to +1.0), negative (to − 1.0), or nonexistent (0.0). In a positive correlation, the values of the variables increase or decrease ("co-vary") together. In a negative correlation, one variable increases as the other decreases. In a nonexistent correlation, no relationship exists between the variables.

People commonly confuse correlation with causation. Correlational data do not indicate *cause-and-effect* relationships. When a correlation exists, changes in the value of one variable reflect changes in the value of the other. The correlation does not imply that one variable causes the other, only that both variables somehow relate to one another. To study the effects that variables have on each other, an investigator must conduct an experiment.

Experimental research

Experimental research attempts to determine *how* and *why* something happens. Experimental research tests the way in which an **independent variable** (the factor that the scientist manipulates) affects a **dependent variable** (the factor that the scientist observes).

A number of factors can affect the outcome of any type of experimental research. One is finding samples that are random and representative of the population being studied. Another is **experimenter bias**, in which the researcher's expectations about what should or should not happen in the study sway the results. Still another is controlling for **extraneous variables**, such as room temperature or noise level, that may interfere with the results of the experiment. Only when the experimenter carefully controls for extraneous variables can she or he draw valid conclusions about the effects of specific variables on other variables.

Cross-cultural research

Sensitivity to others' norms, folkways, values, mores, attitudes, customs, and practices necessitates knowledge of other societies and cultures. Sociologists may conduct **cross-cultural research**, or research designed to reveal variations across different groups of people. Most cross-cultural research involves survey, direct observation, and **participant observation** methods of research.

Participant observation requires that an "observer" become a member of his or her subjects' community. An advantage of this method of research is the opportunity it provides to study what actually occurs within a community, and then consider that information within the political, economic, social, and religious systems of that community. Cross-cultural research demonstrates that Western cultural standards do not necessarily apply to other societies. What may be "normal" or acceptable for one group may be "abnormal" or unacceptable for another.

Research with existing data, or secondary analysis

Some sociologists conduct research by using data that other social scientists have already collected. The use of publicly accessible information is known as **secondary analysis**, and is most common in situations in which collecting new data is impractical or unnecessary. Sociologists may obtain statistical data for analysis from businesses, academic institutions, and governmental agencies, to name only a few sources. Or they may use historical or library information to generate their hypotheses.

Research Ethics

Ethics are self-regulatory guidelines for making decisions and defining professions. By establishing ethical codes, professional organizations maintain the integrity of the profession, define the expected conduct of members, and protect the welfare of subjects and clients. Moreover, ethical codes give professionals direction when confronting **ethical dilemmas**, or confusing situations. A case in point is a scientist's decision whether to intentionally deceive subjects or inform them about the true risks or goals of a controversial but much-needed experiment. Many organizations, such as the American Sociological Association and the American Psychological Association, establish ethical principles and guidelines. The vast majority of today's social scientists abide by their respective organizations' ethical principles.

A researcher must remain mindful of her or his ethical responsibilities to participants. A researcher's primary duty is to protect the welfare of the subjects. For example, a researcher whose study requires extensive questioning of volunteers' personal information should screen the subjects beforehand to assure that the questioning will not distress them. A researcher should also inform subjects about their expected roles in the study, the potential risks of participating, and their freedom to withdraw from the study at any time without consequences. Agreeing to participate in a study based on disclosure of this type of information constitutes **informed consent**. After the study is finished, the researcher should provide subjects with complete details about the study. Providing details at the conclusion of an experiment is called **debriefing**.

Many critics believe that no experiment justifies the intentional use of **deception**, or concealing the purpose and procedures of a study from participants. Not only does deception carry the risk of psychologically harming subjects, it reduces the general public's support for research. Proponents, however, view deception as necessary when prior knowledge of a study would sway a subject's responses and invalidate the results. If subjects learn that a study measures attitudes of racial discrimination, they may intentionally try to avoid appearing prejudiced.

Even the most ethical and cautious researcher cannot anticipate every risk associated with participating in a study. But by carefully screening subjects, informing subjects of their rights, giving them as much information as possible before the study, avoiding deception, and debriefing following the study, the researcher can at least minimize the risks of harm to the subjects.

Evaluating Sociological Research

Sources of sociological research—sociology journals and books, national magazine surveys, television, and "tabloids"—vary considerably in the quality of information offered. So properly evaluating research is important when studying sociology. Much accurate information is available, but so is much inaccurate information. Poorly conducted or poorly designed research tends to fuel society's misconceptions about social topics.

Professional journals and periodicals are the most accurate sources of scientific information about sociology. Not only do professional researchers and clinicians contribute the majority of material to these journals, but their peers also review their material. Thus, the quality of the research published tends to be quite high. A few of the many leading sociological journals are *Applied Behavioral Science Review*, *Clinical Sociology Review*, *Family Life Educator*, *Family Relations*, *Feminist Studies*, *Gender and Society*, *The Gerontologist*, *Humanity and Society*, *Journal of Aging Studies*, *Journal of Family Violence*, *Journal of Gerontology*, *Journal of Marriage and Family*, *Marriage and Family Review*, *Practicing Sociologist*, *Qualitative Sociology*, *Sex Roles*, *Sexual Abuse*, *Social Policy*, *Sociologist Practice*, and *Urban Life*.

Popular magazines and television generally do not provide accurate or scientific information about sociology; rather, studies initially reported in these media are usually sensationalistic and/or poorly designed.

Ask and answer the following questions when deciding the validity of a piece of social research:

- Are the sociologists qualified to conduct sociological studies? What are their credentials? Are the sociologists associated with an academic institution, laboratory, or clinic?

- What research method did the sociologists use? What are the advantages and disadvantages of this method? Do the sociologists acknowledge the limitations associated with their particular method(s)?

- Are the questionnaires or tests used both reliable and valid?

- Is the sample gender-biased, consisting of more men than women, or vice versa? Is the sample biased in any other way? Does it include minorities? Is the sample exclusively urban or rural?

- Do the sociologists make generalizations about a larger population? If so, how representative of the larger population is their sample?

- If the research is an experiment, do the researchers have a control group not exposed to the experimental conditions to compare with the experimental group?

- Do the sociologists use the most appropriate statistical tests to analyze data, or do they simply comment on what appear to be patterns?

- Are the conclusions drawn from the data presented in such a way as to acknowledge other possibilities?

- Do any other published studies support or contradict the sociologists' methods or findings?

Of course, this list of questions is not exhaustive. But thinking about these questions should provide a general sense of the kinds of issues necessary to evaluate sociological research.

Culture consists of the beliefs, behaviors, objects, and other characteristics common to the members of a particular group or society. Through culture, people and groups define themselves, conform to society's shared values, and contribute to society. Thus, culture includes many societal aspects: language, customs, values, norms, mores, rules, tools, technologies, products, organizations, and institutions. This latter term **institution** refers to clusters of rules and cultural meanings associated with specific social activities. Common institutions are the family, education, religion, work, and health care.

Popularly speaking, being **cultured** means being well-educated, knowledgeable of the arts, stylish, and well-mannered. **High culture**—generally pursued by the upper class—refers to classical music, theater, fine arts, and other sophisticated pursuits. Members of the upper class can pursue high art because they have **cultural capital**, which means the professional credentials, education, knowledge, and verbal and social skills necessary to attain the "property, power, and prestige" to "get ahead" socially. **Low culture**, or **popular culture**—generally pursued by the working and middle classes—refers to sports, movies, television sitcoms and soaps, and rock music. Remember that sociologists define *culture* differently than they do *cultured*, *high culture*, *low culture*, and *popular culture*.

Sociologists define **society** as the people who interact in such a way as to share a common culture. The **cultural bond** may be ethnic or racial, based on gender, or due to shared beliefs, values, and activities. The term *society* can also have a *geographic* meaning and refer to people who share a common culture in a particular location. For example, people living in arctic climates developed different cultures from those living in desert cultures. In time, a large variety of human cultures arose around the world.

Culture and society are intricately related. A culture consists of the "objects" of a society, whereas a society consists of the people who share a common culture. When the terms *culture* and *society* first acquired their current meanings, most people in the world worked and lived in small groups in the same locale. In today's world of 6 billion people, these terms have lost some of their usefulness because increasing numbers of people interact and share resources globally. Still, people tend to use *culture* and *society* in a more traditional sense: for example, being a part of a "racial culture" within the larger "U.S. society."

A Biological or Social Basis for Human Culture?

The **nature versus nurture** debate continues to rage in the social sciences. When applied to human culture, proponents of the "nature" side of the debate maintain that human genetics creates cultural forms common to people everywhere. Genetic mutations and anomalies, then, give rise to the behavioral and cultural differences encountered across and among human groups. These differences potentially include language, food and clothing preferences, and sexual attitudes, to name just a few. Proponents of the "nurture" side of the debate maintain that humans are a *tabula rasa* (French for "blank slate") upon which everything is learned, including cultural norms. This fundamental debate has given social scientists and others insights into human nature and culture, but no solid conclusions.

More recently, social learning theorists and sociobiologists have added their expertise and opinions to the debate. **Social learning theorists** hold that humans learn social behaviors within social contexts. That is, behavior is not genetically driven but socially learned. On the other hand, **sociobiologists** argue that, because specific behaviors like aggression are common among all human groups, a *natural selection* must exist for these behaviors similar to that for bodily traits like height. Sociobiologists also hold that people whose "selected" behaviors lead to successful social adaptation more likely reproduce and survive. One generation can genetically transmit successful behavioral characteristics to the next generation.

Today, sociologists generally endorse social learning theory to explain the emergence of culture. That is, they believe that specific behaviors result from social factors that activate physiological predispositions, rather than from heredity and **instincts**, which are biologically fixed patterns of behavior. Because humans are social beings, they learn their behaviors (and beliefs, attitudes, preferences, and the like) within a particular culture. Sociologists find evidence for this social learning position when studying **cultural universals**, or features common to all cultures. Although most societies do share some common elements, sociologists have failed to identify a universal human nature that should theoretically produce identical cultures everywhere. Among other things, language, preference for certain types of food, division of labor, methods of socialization, rules of governance, and a system of religion represent typical cultural features across societies. Yet all these are general rather than specific features of culture. For example, all people consume food of one type or another. But some groups eat insects, while others do not. What one culture accepts as "normal" may vary considerably from what another culture accepts.

Material and Non-Material Culture

Sociologists describe two interrelated aspects of human culture: the physical objects of the culture and the ideas associated with these objects.

Material culture refers to the physical objects, resources, and spaces that people use to define their culture. These include homes, neighborhoods, cities, schools, churches, synagogues, temples, mosques, offices, factories and plants, tools, means of production,

goods and products, stores, and so forth. All of these physical aspects
of a culture help to define its members' behaviors and perceptions.
For example, technology is a vital aspect of material culture in
today's United States. American students must learn to use computers to survive in college and business, in contrast to young adults in
the Yanomamo society in the Amazon who must learn to build
weapons and hunt.

Non-material culture refers to the nonphysical ideas that people have about their culture, including beliefs, values, rules, norms,
morals, language, organizations, and institutions. For instance, the
non-material cultural concept of *religion* consists of a set of ideas and
beliefs about God, worship, morals, and ethics. These beliefs, then,
determine how the culture responds to its religious topics, issues, and
events.

When considering non-material culture, sociologists refer to several processes that a culture uses to shape its members' thoughts, feelings, and behaviors. Four of the most important of these are symbols,
language, values, and norms.

Symbols and Language

To the human mind, **symbols** are cultural representations of reality.
Every culture has its own set of symbols associated with different
experiences and perceptions. Thus, as a representation, a symbol's
meaning is neither instinctive nor automatic. The culture's members
must interpret and over time reinterpret the symbol.

Symbols occur in different forms: verbal or nonverbal, written or
unwritten. They can be anything that conveys a meaning, such as
words on the page, drawings, pictures, and gestures. Clothing, homes,
cars, and other consumer items are symbols that imply a certain level
of social status.

Perhaps the most powerful of all human symbols is **language**—a system of verbal and sometimes written representations that are culturally specific and convey meaning about the world. In the 1930s, **Edward Sapir** and **Benjamin Lee Whorf** proposed that languages influence perceptions. While this Sapir-Whorf hypothesis—also called the **linguistic relativity hypothesis**—is controversial, it legitimately suggests that a person will more likely perceive differences when he or she possesses words or concepts to describe the differences.

Language is an important source of continuity and identity in a culture. Some groups, such as the French-speaking residents of Quebec in Canada, refuse to speak English, which is Canada's primary language, for fear of losing their cultural identity. In the United States, immigrants provide much resistance to making English the official national language.

Values

A culture's **values** are its ideas about what is good, right, fair, and just. Sociologists disagree, however, on how to conceptualize values. Conflict theory focuses on how values differ between groups within a culture, while functionalism focuses on the shared values within a culture. For example, American sociologist **Robert K. Merton** suggested that the most important values in American society are wealth, success, power, and prestige, but that everyone does not have an equal opportunity to attain these values. Functional sociologist **Talcott Parsons** noted that Americans share the common value of the "American work ethic," which encourages hard work. Other sociologists have proposed a common core of American values, including accomplishment, material success, problem-solving, reliance on science and technology, democracy, patriotism, charity, freedom, equality and justice, individualism, responsibility, and accountability.

A culture, though, may harbor conflicting values. For instance, the value of material success may conflict with the value of charity. Or the value of equality may conflict with the value of individualism. Such contradictions may exist due to an inconsistency between people's actions and their professed values, which explains why sociologists must carefully distinguish between what people do and what they say. **Real culture** refers to the values and norms that a society actually follows, while **ideal culture** refers to the values and norms that a society professes to believe.

Norms

Norms are the agreed-upon expectations and rules by which a culture guides the behavior of its members in any given situation. Of course, norms vary widely across cultural groups. Americans, for instance, maintain fairly direct eye contact when conversing with others. Asians, on the other hand, may avert their eyes as a sign of politeness and respect.

Sociologists speak of at least four types of norms: *folkways*, *mores*, *taboos*, and *laws*. **Folkways**, sometimes known as "conventions" or "customs," are standards of behavior that are socially approved but not morally significant. For example, belching loudly after eating dinner at someone else's home breaks an American folkway. **Mores** are norms of morality. Breaking mores, like attending church in the nude, will offend most people of a culture. Certain behaviors are considered **taboo**, meaning a culture absolutely forbids them, like incest in U.S. culture. Finally, **laws** are a formal body of rules enacted by the state and backed by the power of the state. Virtually all taboos, like child abuse, are enacted into law, although not all mores are. For example, wearing a bikini to church may be offensive, but it is not against the law.

Members of a culture must conform to its norms for the culture to exist and function. Hence, members must want to conform and obey rules. They first must internalize the social norms and values that dictate what is "normal" for the culture; then they must **socialize**, or teach norms and values to, their children. If internalization and socialization fail to produce conformity, some form of "social control" is eventually needed. Social control may take the form of ostracism, fines, punishments, and even imprisonment.

Cultural Diversity

Many people mistakenly use such phrases as "American culture," "white culture," or "Western culture," as if such large, common, and homogenous cultures exist in the United States today. These people fail to acknowledge the presence of **cultural diversity**, or the presence of multiple cultures and cultural differences within a society. In reality, many different cultural groups comprise the United States.

Subcultures

Smaller cultural groups that exist within but differ in some way from the prevailing culture interest sociologists. These groups are called **subcultures**. Examples of some subcultures include "heavy metal" music devotees, body-piercing and tatoo enthusiasts, motorcycle gang members, and Nazi skinheads. Members of subcultures typically make use of distinctive language, behaviors, and clothing, even though they may still accept many of the values of the dominant culture.

Ethnic groups living in the United States—such as Greek Americans, Italian Americans, Irish Americans, Mexican Americans, and African Americans—may also form subcultures. Most of these adjust to mainstream America, but may still retain many of their cultural customs and in some cases their native ethnic language.

Countercultures

A **counterculture** comes about in opposition to the norms and values of the dominant culture. Members of countercultures—such as hippies and protest groups—are generally teenagers and young adults, because youth is often a time of identity crisis and experimentation. In time many, but not all, members of countercultures eventually adopt the norms and values of the dominant culture.

Assimilation and multiculturalism

Many people see the United States as "a melting pot" comprised of a variety of different cultural, subcultural, and countercultural groups. When the mainstream absorbs these groups, they have undergone **assimilation**. However, people today increasingly recognize the value of coexisting cultural groups who do not lose their identities.

This perspective of **multiculturalism** respects cultural variations rather than requiring that the dominant culture assimilate the various cultures. It holds that certain shared cultural tenets are important to society as a whole, but that some cultural differences are important, too. For example, children in schools today are being taught that the United States is not the only culture in the world, and that other viewpoints may have something to offer Americans.

Ethnocentrism and cultural relativism

Ethnocentrism involves judging other cultures against the standards of one's own culture. *Norms* within a culture frequently translate into what is considered "normal," so that people think their own way of doing things is "natural." These same people also judge other people's ways of doing things as "unnatural." In other words, they forget that what may be considered normal in America is not necessarily so in another part of the world.

A potentially problematic form of ethnocentrism is **nationalism**, or an overly enthusiastic identification with a particular nation. Nationalism often includes the notion that a particular nation has a God-given or historical claim to superiority. Such nationalism, for instance, was a special problem in World War II Nazi Germany.

Sociologists strive to avoid ethnocentric judgments. Instead, they generally embrace **cultural relativism**, or the perspective that a culture should be sociologically evaluated according to its own standards, and not those of any other culture. Thus, sociologists point out that there really are no good or bad cultures. And they are better able to understand the standards of other cultures because they do not assume their own is somehow better.

Toward a Global Culture

Some sociologists today predict that the world is moving closer to a global culture, void of cultural diversity. A fundamental means by which cultures come to resemble each other is via the phenomenon of **cultural diffusion**, or the spreading of standards across cultures. Cultures have always influenced each other through travel, trade, and even conquest. As populations today travel and settle around the globe, however, the rate of cultural diffusion is increasing dramatically. Examples of social forces that are creating a global culture include electronic communications (telephones, e-mail, fax machines), the mass media (television, radio, film), the news media, the Internet, international businesses and banks, and the United Nations—to name only a few. Even phrases like "global village" seem to imply that the world is growing "smaller" every day.

Still, while many aspects of culture have been globalized, local societies and cultures remain stable and, in many instances, are being affirmed with enthusiasm. Although people may relocate on the other side of the planet, they tend to remain faithful to their culture of origin.

Types of Societies

Although humans have established many types of societies throughout history, sociologists and anthropologists (experts who study early
and tribal cultures) usually refer to six basic types of societies, each
defined by its level of technology.

Hunting and gathering societies
The members of **hunting and gathering societies** primarily survive
by hunting animals, fishing, and gathering plants. The vast majority
of these societies existed in the past, with only a few (perhaps a million people total) living today on the verge of extinction.

To survive, early human societies completely depended upon
their immediate environment. When the animals left the area, the
plants died, or the rivers dried up, the society had to relocate to an
area where resources were plentiful. Consequently, hunting and gathering societies, which were typically small, were quite mobile. In
some cases, where resources in a locale were extraordinarily plentiful, small villages might form. But most hunting and gathering societies were **nomadic**, moving constantly in search of food and water.

Labor in hunting and gathering societies was divided equally
among members. Because of the mobile nature of the society, these
societies stored little in the form of surplus goods. Therefore, anyone
who could hunt, fish, or gather fruits and vegetables did so. These
societies probably also had at least some division of labor based on
gender. Males probably traveled long distances to hunt and capture
larger animals. Females hunted smaller animals, gathered plants,
made clothing, protected and raised children, and helped the males
to protect the community from rival groups.

Hunting and gathering societies were also **tribal**. Members shared
an ancestral heritage and a common set of traditions and rituals. They
also sacrificed their individuality for the sake of the larger tribal culture.

Pastoral societies

Members of **pastoral societies**, which first emerged 12,000 years ago, pasture animals for food and transportation. Pastoral societies still exist today, primarily in the desert lands of North Africa where horticulture and manufacturing are not possible.

Domesticating animals allows for a more manageable food supply than do hunting and gathering. Hence, pastoral societies are able to produce a surplus of goods, which makes storing food for future use a possibility. With storage comes the desire to develop settlements that permit the society to remain in a single place for longer periods of time. And with stability comes the trade of surplus goods between neighboring pastoral communities.

Pastoral societies allow certain of its members (those who are not domesticating animals) to engage in nonsurvival activities. Traders, healers, spiritual leaders, craftspeople, and people with other specialty professions appear.

Horticultural societies

Unlike pastoral societies that rely on domesticating animals, **horticultural societies** rely on cultivating fruits, vegetables, and plants. These societies first appeared in different parts of the planet about the same time as pastoral societies. Like hunting and gathering societies, horticultural societies had to be mobile. Depletion of the land's resources or dwindling water supplies, for example, forced the people to leave. Horticultural societies occasionally produced a surplus, which permitted storage as well as the emergence of other professions not related to the survival of the society.

Agricultural societies

Agricultural societies use technological advances to cultivate crops (especially grains like wheat, rice, corn, and barley) over a large area. Sociologists use the phrase **Agricultural Revolution** to refer to the technological changes that occurred as long as 8,500 years ago that led to cultivating crops and raising farm animals. Increases in food supplies then led to larger populations than in earlier communities. This meant a greater surplus, which resulted in towns that became centers of trade supporting various rulers, educators, craftspeople, merchants, and religious leaders who did not have to worry about locating nourishment.

Greater degrees of social stratification appeared in agricultural societies. For example, women previously had higher social status because they shared labor more equally with men. In hunting and gathering societies, women even gathered more food than men. But as food stores improved and women took on lesser roles in providing food for the family, they became more subordinate to men.

As villages and towns expanded into neighboring areas, conflicts with other communities inevitably occurred. Farmers provided warriors with food in exchange for protection against invasion by enemies. A system of rulers with high social status also appeared. This **nobility** organized warriors to protect the society from invasion. In this way, the nobility managed to extract goods from the "lesser" persons of society.

Feudal societies

From the 9th to 15th centuries, **feudalism** was a form of society based on ownership of land. Unlike today's farmers, *vassals* under feudalism were bound to cultivating their lord's land. In exchange for military protection, the lords exploited the peasants into providing food, crops, crafts, homage, and other services to the owner of the land. The *caste* system of feudalism was often multigenerational; the families of peasants may have cultivated their lord's land for generations.

Between the 14th and 16th centuries, a new economic system emerged that began to replace feudalism. **Capitalism** is marked by open competition in a free market, in which the means of production are privately owned. Europe's exploration of the Americas served as one impetus for the development of capitalism. The introduction of foreign metals, silks, and spices stimulated great commercial activity in Europe.

Industrial societies
Industrial societies are based on using machines (particularly fuel-driven ones) to produce goods. Sociologists refer to the period during the 18th century when the production of goods in mechanized factories began as the **Industrial Revolution**. The Industrial Revolution appeared first in Britain, and then quickly spread to the rest of the world.

As productivity increased, means of transportation improved to better facilitate the transfer of products from place to place. Great wealth was attained by the few who owned factories, and the "masses" found jobs working in the factories.

Industrialization brought about changes in almost every aspect of society. As factories became the center of work, "home cottages" as the usual workplace became less prevalent, as did the family's role in providing vocational training and education. Public education via schools and eventually the mass media became the norm. People's life expectancy increased as their health improved. Political institutions changed into modern models of governance. Cultural diversity increased, as did social mobility. Large cities emerged as places to find jobs in factories. Social power moved into the hands of business elites and governmental officials, leading to struggles between industrialists and workers. Labor unions and welfare organizations formed in response to these disputes and concerns over workers' welfare, including children who toiled in factories. Rapid changes in industrial technology also continued, especially the production of larger machines and faster means of transportation. The Industrial Revolution also saw to the development of **bureaucratic** forms of organization, complete with written rules, job descriptions, impersonal positions, and hierarchical methods of management.

Postindustrial societies

Sociologists note that with the advent of the computer microchip, the world is witnessing a technological revolution. This revolution is creating a **postindustrial society** based on information, knowledge, and the selling of services. That is, rather than being driven by the factory production of goods, society is being shaped by the human mind, aided by computer technology. Although factories will always exist, the key to wealth and power seems to lie in the ability to generate, store, manipulate, and sell information.

Sociologists speculate about the characteristics of postindustrial society in the near future. They predict increased levels of education and training, consumerism, availability of goods, and social mobility. While they hope for a decline in inequality as technical skills and "know-how" begin to determine class rather than the ownership of property, sociologists are also concerned about potential social divisions based on those who have appropriate education and those who do not. Sociologists believe society will become more concerned with the welfare of all members of society. They hope postindustrial society will be less characterized by social conflict, as everyone works together to solve society's problems through science.

Socialization is the process whereby infants and children *develop* into social beings. Among other things, children develop a sense of self, memory, language, and intellect. And in doing so, they learn from their elders the attitudes, values, and proper social behaviors of the culture into which they were born. Becoming socialized benefits the individual by giving him or her the tools needed for success in the native culture, and also benefits the society by providing continuity over time and preserving its essential nature from generation to generation. In other words, socialization connects different generations to each other.

"Unsocialized" Children

Stories of children found after years of living in the "wild" without any human contact occasionally appear in the literature. One of the most commonly cited examples is the *Boy of Aveyron* who emerged little more than a "beast" from a forest in France in 1798. "Unsocialized" children such as this boy typically look more animal than human, prefer to remain naked (at least at first upon being discovered), lack human speech, have no sense of personal hygiene, fail to recognize themselves in a mirror, show little or no reasoning ability, and respond only partially to attempts to help them change from "animal into human." The phenomenon of **feral** (literally *wild* or untamed) children sparks much discussion regarding the **nature versus nurture debate** (see Chapter 1), because research shows that the state of these children seems to suggest the important role that learning plays in normal human development.

Social scientists emphasize that socialization is intimately related to *cognitive, personality, and social development.* They argue that socialization primarily occurs during infancy and childhood, although they acknowledge that humans continue to grow and adapt throughout the lifespan. Sociologists also refer to the driving forces behind socialization as **socializing agents**, which include family, friends, peers, school, work, the mass media, and religion.

Piaget's Model of Cognitive Development

Much of modern cognitive theory, including its relationship to socialization, stems from the work of the Swiss psychologist, **Jean Piaget**. In the 1920s Piaget observed children reasoning and understanding differently, depending on their age. He proposed that all children progress through a series of cognitive stages of development, just as they progress through a series of physical stages of development. According to Piaget, the rate at which children pass through these cognitive stages may vary, but they eventually pass through all of them in the same order.

Piaget introduced several other important concepts. According to Piaget, cognitive development occurs from two processes: adaptation and equilibrium. **Adaptation** involves the child's changing to meet situational demands. Adaptation involves two sub-processes: assimilation and accommodation. **Assimilation** is the application of previous concepts to new concepts. An example is the child who refers to a whale as a "fish." **Accommodation** is the altering of previous concepts in the face of new information. An example is the child who discovers that some creatures living in the ocean are not fish, and then correctly refers to a whale as a "mammal." **Equilibrium** is the search for "balance" between self and the world, and involves the matching of the child's adaptive functioning to situational demands. Equilibrium keeps the infant moving along the developmental pathway, allowing him or her to make increasingly effective adaptations.

A brief summary of Piaget's four stages of cognitive development appears in Table 4-1.

Table 4-1: Piaget's Stages of Cognitive Development

Stage	Age	Characteristics of Stage
Sensorimotor	0–2	The child learns by doing: looking, touching, sucking. The child also has a primitive understanding of cause-and-effect relationships. Object permanence appears around 9 months.
Preoperational	2–7	The child uses language and symbols, including letters and numbers. Egocentrism is also evident. Conservation marks the end of the preoperational stage and the beginning of concrete operations.
Concrete Operations	7–11	The child demonstrates conservation, reversibility, serial ordering, and a mature understanding of cause-and-effect relationships. Thinking at this stage is still concrete.
Formal Operations	12+	The individual demonstrates abstract thinking, including logic, deductive reasoning, comparison, and classification.

Cognitive Development in Infancy,
Toddlerhood, and Early Childhood (0–6)

During Piaget's **sensorimotor stage** (birth to age 2), infants and toddlers learn by doing: looking, hearing, touching, grasping, sucking. The process appears to begin with primitive "thinking" that involves coordinating movements of the body with incoming sensory data. As infants intentionally attempt to interact with the environment, they learn that certain actions lead to specific consequences. This is the beginning of the infants' understanding of cause-and-effect relationships.

Piaget referred to the cognitive development occurring between ages 2 and 7 as the **preoperational stage**. In this stage, children increase their use of language and other symbols, imitation of adult behaviors, and play. Young children develop a fascination with words—both "good" and "bad." They also play "pretend" games. Piaget also described this stage in terms of what children cannot do. He used the term **operational** to refer to *reversible abilities* that children had not yet developed. By **reversible**, Piaget meant actions that children perform in their mind, but that can occur in either direction. Adding (3 + 3 = 6) and subtracting (6 − 3 = 3) are examples of reversible actions.

Piaget believed that **egocentrism**—the inability to distinguish between one's own point of view and those of others—limits preschoolers' cognitive abilities. The capacity for egocentricity exists at all stages of cognitive development, but becomes particularly apparent during the preschool years. Young children eventually overcome this early form of egocentrism when they learn that others have different views, feelings, and desires. Then they can interpret other's motives, and use those interpretations to communicate mutually— and therefore more effectively—with others. Preschoolers eventually learn to adjust their vocal pitch, tone, and speed to match those of the listener. Because mutual communication requires effort and preschoolers are still egocentric, they may lapse into egocentric speech (non-mutual) during times of frustration. That is, children may **regress** to earlier behavioral patterns when their cognitive resources become stressed and overwhelmed.

Piaget also believed that young children cannot grasp the concept of **conservation**, which is the concept that physical properties remain constant even as appearance and form changes. They have trouble understanding that the same amount of liquid poured into containers of different shapes remains the same. A preoperational child will tell you that a short, fat bottle does not contain the same amount of liquid as a tall skinny one. Similarly, a preoperational child will tell you that a handful of pennies is more money than a single five-dollar bill. When children develop the cognitive capacity to conserve at around age 7, according to Piaget they move into the next stage of development, **concrete operations**.

Cognitive Development in Middle Childhood (7–11)

Piaget referred to the cognitive development occurring between ages 7 and 11 as the **concrete operations stage**. While in concrete operations, children cannot think logically and abstractly. They are limited to thinking "concretely," or in tangible, definite, exact, and uni-directional terms based on real and concrete experiences rather than on logical abstractions. These children do not use "magical thinking," so they are not as easily misled as younger children.

Piaget noted that children's thinking changes significantly during the concrete operations stage. They can engage in **classification**, which is the ability to group according to features, and **serial ordering**, which is the ability to group according to logical progression. Older children come to understand cause-and-effect relationships, so they become adept at mathematics and science. They also comprehend the concept of stable **identity**—that "self" remains constant even when circumstances change. For example, older children know that their father maintains a male identity regardless of what he wears or how old he becomes.

In Piaget's view, children at the beginning of concrete operations do demonstrate conservation. Unlike preschoolers, school-age children understand that the same amount of clay molded into different shapes remains the same. Children in concrete operations have also advanced beyond the egocentrism of preschoolers. By the school years, children have usually learned that other people have their own views, feelings, and desires.

Cognitive Development in Adolescence (12+)

Most adolescents reach Piaget's stage of **formal operations** (ages 12 and older), in which they develop new tools for manipulating information. Previously as children, they could only think concretely. But now in formal operations, they can think abstractly and deductively. Adolescents in this stage can also consider future possibilities, search for answers, deal flexibly with problems, test hypotheses, and draw conclusions about events they have not experienced first-hand.

Cognitive maturity occurs as the brain matures and the social network expands, offering more opportunities for experimenting with life. Because this worldly experience plays a large role in attaining formal operations, not all adolescents enter this stage of cognitive development. Studies indicate, however, that abstract and critical reasoning skills are teachable. For example, everyday reasoning improves between the first and last years of college, which suggests the value of education in cognitive maturation.

Social and Personality Development in Infancy and Toddlerhood

During infancy and toddlerhood, children easily attach to others. They normally form their initial primary relationship with their parents and other family members. Because infants depend completely on their parents for food, clothing, warmth, and nurturing, Erik Erikson noted that the primary task during this first **psychosocial** stage of life is to learn to **trust** (rather than to **mistrust**) the caregivers. The child's first few years—including forming relationships and developing an organized sense of self—set the stage for both immediate and later psychosocial development, including the emergence of **prosocial behavior**, or the capacity to help, cooperate, and share with others. (Table 4-2 contrasts Erikson's model of psychosocial development with Sigmund Freud's model.)

Table 4-2: Contrasting Models of Psychosocial Development

Period (Age)	Freud's Stage	Erikson's Task or Crisis
Infancy (0–1)	Oral	Trust vs. mistrust
Toddlerhood and early childhood (1–3)	Anal	Autonomy vs. shame
Early childhood (3–6)	Phallic	Initiative vs. guilt
Middle childhood (7–11)	Latency	Industry vs. inferiority
Adolescence (12–19)	Genital	Identity vs. confusion
Early adulthood (20–45)		Intimacy vs. isolation
Middle adulthood (45–65)		Generativity vs. stagnation
Late adulthood (65+)		Integrity vs. despair

Personality includes those stable psychological characteristics that define each human being as unique. Both children and adults evidence personality **traits** (long-term characteristics, such as temperament) and **states** (changeable characteristics, such as moodiness). While considerable debate continues over the etiology of personality, most experts agree that personality traits and states form early in life. A combination of genetics and psychological and social influences likely influence the formation of personality.

Infants are typically **egocentric**, or self-centered. They primarily concern themselves with satisfying their physical desires (for example, hunger), which psychoanalyst **Sigmund Freud** theorized is a form of self-pleasuring. Because infants are particularly interested in activities involving the mouth (sucking, biting), Freud labeled the first year of life as the **oral stage** of **psychosexual development**. (Freud's model of psychosexual development appears in Table 4-2.)

According to Freud, too little or too much stimulation of a particular **erogenous zone** (sensitive area of the body) at a particular psychosexual stage of development leads to **fixation** (literally, being "stuck") at that stage. Multiple fixations are possible at multiple stages. In the case of infants, fixation at the oral stage gives rise to adult personality traits centered around the mouth. Adult "oral focused habits" may take the form of overeating, drinking, and smoking. Adults are especially prone to "regressing" to such childhood fixation behaviors during times of stress and upset.

Theorists after Freud have offered additional perspectives on infant personality development. Perhaps the most important of these is **Melanie Klein's object-relations theory**. According to Klein, the inner core of personality stems from the early relationship with the mother. While Freud speculated that the child's fear of a powerful father determines personality, Klein speculated that the child's need for a powerful mother plays a more important role. In other words, the child's fundamental human drive is to be in relationship with others, of whom the mother is usually the first.

Klein affirmed that infants bond to objects rather than people, because the infant cannot fully understand what a person is. An infant's very limited perspective can only process an evolving perception of what a person is.

In object-relations theory, girls adjust better psychosocially than boys. Girls become extensions of the mother; they do not need to separate. Boys, on the other hand, must separate from the mother to become independent. This contrasts with Freud's theory, in which boys develop a stronger **superego** (conscious) than girls do because boys have a penis and girls do not. Therefore, boys more easily resolve their **Oedipal conflict** (attraction to the female parent) than girls do their **Electra conflict** (attraction to the male parent).

Family relationships in infancy and toddlerhood

A baby's first relationships are with family members, to whom the infant expresses a range of emotions (and vice versa). If the social and emotional bonding fails in some way, the child may never develop the trust, self-control, or emotional reasoning necessary to function effectively in the world. The quality of the relationship between child and parents—especially between months 6 and 18— seems to determine the quality of the child's later relationships.

If physical contact between infant and parents plays such a vital role in the emotional health of the infant, and is important to the parents as well, when should such contact begin? Most experts recommend that physical contact occur as soon as possible after delivery. Studies show that babies who receive immediate maternal contact seem to cry less and are happier and more secure than babies who do not. Immediate bonding is optimal, but infants and parents can later make up for an initial separation.

Attachment

Attachment is the process whereby one individual seeks nearness to another individual. In parent-child interactions, attachment is mutual and reciprocal. The infant looks and smiles at the parents, who look and smile at the infant. Communication between child and parents is indeed basic at this level, but it is also profound.

Psychologist **John Bowlby** suggested that infants are born "preprogrammed" for certain behaviors that will guarantee bonding with the caregivers. The infant's crying, clinging, smiling, and "cooing" are designed to prompt parental feeding, holding, cuddling, and vocalizing. Parents can help instill trust in their infant as the child forms attachments. Eye contact, touching, and timely feedings are perhaps the most important ways. These, of course, also represent expressions of the love and affection parents have for their children.

Attachment is central to human existence, but so are separation and loss. Ultimately, relationships are interrupted, or they dissolve on their own. Children must learn that nothing human is permanent, though learning this concept is not as easy as it may first sound. According to Bowlby, children who are separated from their parents progress through three stages: protest, despair, and detachment. After first refusing to accept the separation, and then losing hope, the child finally accepts the separation and begins to respond to the attention of new caregivers.

Social deprivation, or the absence of attachment, produces profoundly negative effects on children. For instance, children who have been institutionalized without close or continuous attachments for long periods of time display pathological levels of depression, withdrawal, apathy, and anxiety.

Parenting in infancy and toddlerhood

Cultural and community standards, the social environment, and their children's behavior determine parents' child-raising practices. Hence different parents have different ideas on responding to their children, communicating with them, and placing them into daycare.

Responding (for example, playing, vocalizing, feeding, touching) to an infant's needs is certainly important to the child's psychosocial development. In fact, children who display strong attachment tend to have highly responsive mothers. Does this mean that the caregivers should respond to everything an infant does? Probably not. Children must learn that all needs cannot be completely met all the time. The majority of caregivers respond *most of the time* to their infants, but not 100 percent of the time. Problems only seem to arise when primary caregivers respond to infants less than 25 percent of the time. The children of "nonresponding" mothers tend to be insecurely attached, which may lead to simultaneous over-dependence upon and rejection of authority figures later in adulthood.

Strong communication between parents and children leads to strong attachment and relationships. **Mutuality**, or "synchronous" interaction, particularly during the first few months, predicts a secure relationship between parents and infants. Mutual behaviors include taking turns approaching and withdrawing, looking and touching, and "talking" to each other.

With the first few months and years being so critical to children's future psychosocial development, some parents worry about having to place their infants and toddlers in daycare and preschool. Research suggests that children who attend daycare while both parents work are not at a disadvantage regarding development of self, prosocial behavior, or cognitive functioning. Many authorities argue that daycare, coupled with *quality* time with the parents whenever possible, provides better and earlier socialization than may otherwise occur.

Social and Personality Development in Early Childhood

During early childhood, children gain some sense of being separate and independent from their parents. According to Erikson, the task of preschoolers is to develop **autonomy**, or **self-direction** (ages 1–3), as well as **initiative**, or **enterprise** (ages 3–6).

According to Freud, children in the second year of life enter the **anal stage** of psychosexual development, when parents face many new challenges while toilet training their children. Fixations at this stage give rise to the characteristic personality traits of *anal retention* (excessive neatness, organization, and withholding) or *anal expulsion* (messiness and altruism), which fully emerge in adulthood.

Family relationships are critical to the physical, mental, and social health of growing preschoolers. Many aspects of the family, such as parenting techniques, discipline, the number and the birth order of siblings, the family's finances, the family's circumstances, the family's health, and more, contribute to young children's psychosocial development.

Parenting in early childhood
Different parents employ different parenting techniques. Which parents choose to use which techniques depends on cultural and community standards, the situation, and their children's behavior at the time. **Parental control** involves the degree to which parents are restrictive in their use of parenting techniques, while **parental warmth** involves the degree to which they are loving, affectionate, and approving in their use of these techniques.

- **Authoritarian parents** demonstrate high parental control and low parental warmth when parenting.

- **Permissive parents** demonstrate high parental warmth and low parental control when parenting.

- **Indifferent parents** demonstrate low parental control and low warmth.

- **Authoritative parents** demonstrate appropriate levels of both parental control and warmth.

The willingness of parents to negotiate common goals with their children is highly desirable. This does not imply, however, that everything within a family system is negotiable. Neither parents nor their children should be "in charge" all of the time. Doing so can lead to unhealthy power struggles within the family. Parental negotiating teaches children that quality relationships can be **equitable**, or equal in terms of sharing rights, responsibilities, and decision-making. Most negotiating home environments are warm, accommodating, and mutually supportive.

Siblings in early childhood

Siblings form a child's first and foremost peer group. Preschoolers may learn as much or more from their siblings as from their parents. Regardless of age differences, sibling relationships mirror other social relationships, amounting to a type of basic preparation for dealing with people outside of the home. Only brothers and sisters can simultaneously have equal and unequal status in the home, and only they can provide opportunities (whether desired or not) to practice coping with the positives and negatives of human relationships.

Are "only children" (those without siblings) at a developmental disadvantage? *No.* Research confirms that "onlies" perform just as well as, if not better than, other children on measures of personality, intelligence, and achievement. One explanation is that, like children who are first in the birth order, "only children" may receive the undivided (or nearly undivided) attention of their parents, who in turn have more time to read to them, take them to museums, and encourage them to excel.

Friends and playmates in early childhood

Early family attachments may determine the ease with which children form friendships and other relationships. Children who have loving, stable, and accepting relationships with their parents and siblings are generally more likely to find the same in friends and playmates.

First friends appear at about age 3, though preschoolers may play together long before that age. Much like adults, children tend to develop friends who share common interests, are likable, offer support, and are similar in size and looks.

Childhood friends offer opportunities to learn how to handle anger-provoking situations, to share, to learn values, and to practice more "grown-up" behaviors. Preschoolers who are popular with their peers excel at these activities. Those who are not popular may benefit from adult interventions that encourage them to be less shy and more social.

Social and Personality Development in Middle Childhood

Erikson's primary developmental task of middle childhood is to attain **industry**, or the feeling of social competence. Competition (for example, athletics and daredevil activities) and numerous social adjustments (trying to make and keep friends) mark this developmental stage. Successfully developing industry helps the child build **self-esteem**, which in turn builds the self-confidence necessary to form lasting and effective social relationships.

Self-concept in middle childhood

Most boys and girls in middle childhood develop a positive sense of self-understanding, self-definition, and self-control, especially when their parents, teachers, and friends demonstrate regard for and emotionally support them, and when children themselves feel competent. When lacking in one social area, children in this age group typically find another area in which to excel, which contributes to an overall sense of self-esteem and belonging in the social world. For example, a child who does not like math may take up the piano as a hobby. The more positive experiences children have excelling, the more likely they will develop the self-confidence necessary to confront new social challenges. Self-esteem, self-worth, self-regulation, and self-confidence ultimately form the child's **self-concept**.

Social cognition in middle childhood

As children grow up, they improve in their use of **social cognition**, or experiential knowledge and understanding of society and the "rules of life." They also improve in their use of **social inferences**, or assumptions about the nature of social relationships and processes, as well as of others' feelings. Peer relationships play a major role in fine-tuning social cognition in middle childhood. Members of a child's peer group typically come from the same race and socioeconomic status.

Noncompetitive activities among peers help children to develop quality relationships, while competitive ones help them to discover unique aspects of themselves. Thus, as children in middle childhood interact with their peers, they learn trust and honesty, as well as how to have rewarding social relationships. Eventually, teenagers' social cognition comes to fruition as they form long-term relationships based on trust. Throughout these experiences, children come to grips with the world as a social environment with regulations. In time they become better at predicting what is socially appropriate and workable, as well as what is not.

Family relationships in middle childhood

Even though school-age children spend more time away from home than they did as younger children, their most important relationships remain in the home. These children normally enjoy the company of their parents, grandparents, siblings, and extended family members.

Middle childhood is a transitional stage—a time of sharing power and decision-making with the parents. Yet parents must continue to establish rules and define boundaries because children have only limited experiences upon which to draw when dealing with adult situations and issues.

This period is also a time of increased responsibility for children. In addition to allowing increased freedom (such as going unsupervised to the Saturday afternoon movies with their peers), parents may assign their children additional household chores (watching their younger siblings after school while the parents work). The majority of school-age children appreciate their parents' acceptance of their more "adult-like" role in the family.

Discipline, while not necessarily synonymous with punishment, remains an issue in middle childhood. The question, which has been debated in social science circles for decades, becomes one of discipline's role in teaching children values, morals, integrity, and self-control. Most authorities today agree that punishment is probably of less value than **positive reinforcement**, or rewarding acceptable behaviors. Some parents choose to use both discipline and positive reinforcement techniques with their children.

Most families today require two incomes to make ends meet. Consequently, some children express negative feelings about being "latchkey kids" while both parents work. Children may question why their parents "choose" to spend so little time with them. Or they may become resentful at not being greeted after school by one or both parents. Straightforward and honest communication between parents and children can do much to alleviate any concerns or upset that may arise. Parents can remind their children that the *quality* of time spent together is more important than the *quantity* of time.

Friends and playmates in middle childhood
Friendships, especially same-gender ones, are prevalent during middle childhood. Friends serve as classmates, comrades, fellow adventurers, confidantes, and "sounding boards." They also help each other to develop self-esteem and a sense of competency in the social world. As boys and girls progress through middle childhood, their peer relationships take on greater importance. This means that older children likely enjoy group activities such as skating, riding bikes, playing house, and building forts. This also means popularity and conformity become the focus of intense concern and even worry.

Similar to same-age peers, friendships in middle childhood are mostly based on similarity and may or may not be affected by the awareness of racial or other differences. Intolerance for those who are dissimilar leads to **prejudice**, or negative perceptions about those who are different. Although peers and friends may reinforce prejudicial stereotypes, many children eventually become less rigid in their thinking about children from different backgrounds.

Many sociologists consider **peer pressure** a negative consequence of peer friendships and relationships. Those children most susceptible to peer pressure typically have low self-esteem. They in turn adopt the group's "norms" as their own in an attempt to enhance their self-esteem. When children cannot resist the influence of their peers, particularly in ambiguous situations, they may begin smoking, drinking, stealing, or lying if their peers encourage such behaviors.

Social and Personality Development in Adolescence

Adolescence is the period of transition between childhood and adulthood. Social scientists have traditionally viewed adolescence as a time of psychosocial "storm and stress"—of bearing the burdens of wanting to be an adult long before becoming one. Sociologists today are more likely to view adolescence as a positive time of opportunities and growth, as most adolescents traverse this transition without serious problems or rifts with parents.

Freud called the period of psychosexual development beginning with puberty the **genital stage**. During this stage sexual development reaches adult maturity, resulting in a healthy ability to love and work if the individual has successfully progressed through previous stages. Because early pioneers in development concerned themselves only with childhood, Freud explained that the genital stage encompasses all of adulthood, and described no special difference between adolescent and adult years.

In contrast, Erikson noted that the chief conflict facing the adolescent at this stage is one of **identity versus identity confusion**. Hence, the adolescent is posed with the psychosocial task of developing individuality. To form an identity, adolescents must define personal roles in society and integrate the various dimensions of their personalities into a sensible whole. They must wrestle with such issues as selecting a career, college, religious system, and political party.

Researchers **Carol Gilligan** and **Deborah Tannen** have found differences in the ways in which males and females achieve identity. Gilligan has noted that females seek intimate relationships, while males seek independence and achievement. Deborah Tannen has explained these differences as being due, at least in part, to the dissimilar ways in which parents socialize males and females.

The hormonal changes of puberty affect the emotions of adolescents. Along with emotional and sexual fluctuations comes the need for adolescents to question authority and societal values, as well as to test limits within existing relationships. These needs become readily apparent within the family system, where adolescents' desire for independence from parents and siblings can cause a great deal of conflict and tension at home.

Societal mores and expectations during adolescence restrain the curiosity so characteristic of young children, even though peer pressure to try new things and behave in certain ways is also very powerful. Additionally, teenagers experience a growing desire for personal responsibility and independence from their parents, along with an ever-growing, irresistible interest in sexuality.

Social groups and organizations comprise a basic part of virtually every arena of modern life. Thus, in the last 50 years or so, sociologists have taken a special interest in studying these scientific phenomena from a scientific point of view.

Social Groups

A social **group** is a collection of people who interact with each other and share similar characteristics and a sense of unity. A social **category** is a collection of people who do not interact but who share similar characteristics. For example, women, men, the elderly, and high school students all constitute social categories. A social category can become a social group when the members in the category interact with each other and identify themselves as members of the group. In contrast, a social **aggregate** is a collection of people who are in the same place, but who do not interact or share characteristics.

Psychologists **Muzafer** and **Carolyn Sherif**, in a classic experiment in the 1950s, divided a group of 12-year-old white, middle-class boys at a summer camp into the "Eagles" and the "Rattlers." At first, when the boys did not know one another, they formed a common social category as summer campers. But as time passed and they began to consider themselves to be either Eagles or Rattlers, these 12-year-old boys formed two distinct social groups.

In-groups, out-groups, and reference groups
In the Sherifs' experiment, the youngsters also erected artificial boundaries between themselves. They formed **in-groups** (to which loyalty is expressed) and **out-groups** (to which antagonism is expressed).

To some extent every social group creates boundaries between itself and other groups, but a cohesive in-group typically has three characteristics:

- Members use titles, external symbols, and dress to distinguish themselves from the out-group.

- Members tend to clash or compete with members of the out-group. This competition with the other group can also strengthen the unity within each group.

- Members apply positive stereotypes to their in-group and negative stereotypes to the out-group.

In the beginning, the Eagles and Rattlers were friendly, but soon their games evolved into intense competitions. The two groups began to call each other names, and they raided each other's cabins, hazed one another, and started fights. In other words, loyalty to the in-group led to antagonism and aggression toward the out-group, including fierce competitions for the same resources. Later in the same experiment, though, Sherif had the boys work together to solve mutual problems. When they cooperated with one another, the Eagles and Rattlers became less divided, hostile, and competitive.

People may form opinions or judge their own behaviors against those of a **reference group** (a group used as a standard for self-appraisals). Parishioners at a particular church, for instance, may evaluate themselves by the standards of a denomination, and then feel good about adhering to those standards. Such positive self-evaluation reflects the **normative effect** that a reference group has on its own members, as well as those who compare themselves to the group. Still, reference groups can have a **comparison effect** on self-evaluations. If most parishioners shine in their spiritual accomplishments, then the others will probably compare themselves to them. Consequently, the "not-so-spiritual" parishioners may form a negative self-appraisal for not feeling "up to par." Thus, reference groups can exert a powerful influence on behavior and attitudes.

Primary and secondary groups

Groups play a basic role in the development of the social nature and ideals of people. **Primary groups** are those in which individuals intimately interact and cooperate over a long period of time. Examples of primary groups are families, friends, peers, neighbors, classmates, sororities, fraternities, and church members. These groups are marked by **primary relationships** in which communication is informal. Members of primary groups have strong emotional ties. They also relate to one another as whole and unique individuals.

In contrast, **secondary groups** are those in which individuals do not interact much. Members of secondary groups are less personal or emotional than those of primary groups. These groups are marked by **secondary relationships** in which communication is formal. Members of secondary groups may not know each other or have much face-to-face interaction. They tend to relate to others only in particular roles and for practical reasons. An example of a secondary relationship is that of a stockbroker and her clients. The stockbroker likely relates to her clients in terms of business only. She probably will not socialize with her clients or hug them.

Primary relationships are most common in small and traditional societies, while secondary relationships are the norm in large and industrial societies. Because secondary relationships often result in loneliness and isolation, some members of society may attempt to create primary relationships through singles' groups, dating services, church groups, and communes, to name a few. This does not mean, however, that secondary relationships are bad. For most Americans, time and other commitments limit the number of possible primary relationships. Further, acquaintances and friendships can easily spring forth from secondary relationships.

Small groups

A group's size can also determine how its members behave and relate. A **small group** is small enough to allow all of its members to directly interact. Examples of small groups include families, friends, discussion groups, seminar classes, dinner parties, and athletic teams. People are more likely to experience primary relationships in small group settings than in large settings.

The smallest of small groups is a **dyad** consisting of two people. A dyad is perhaps the most cohesive of all groups because of its potential for very close and intense interactions. It also runs the risk, though, of splitting up. A **triad** is a group consisting of three persons. A triad does not tend to be as cohesive and personal as a dyad.

The more people who join a group, the less personal and intimate that group becomes. In other words, as a group increases in size, its members participate and cooperate less, and are more likely to be dissatisfied. A larger group's members may even be inhibited, for example, from publicly helping out victims in an emergency. In this case, people may feel that because so many others are available to help, responsibility to help is shifted to others. Similarly, as a group increases in size, its members are more likely to engage in **social loafing**, in which people work less because they expect others to take over their tasks.

Leadership and conformity
Sociologists have been especially interested in two forms of group behavior: *conformity* and *leadership*.

The pressure to conform within small groups can be quite powerful. Many people go along with the majority regardless of the consequences or their personal opinions. Nothing makes this phenomenon more apparent than Solomon Asch's classic experiments from the 1950s and 1960s.

Asch assembled several groups of student volunteers and then asked the subjects which of the three lines on a card was as long as the line on another card. Each of the student groups had only one actual subject; the others were Asch's secret accomplices, whom he had instructed to provide the same, though absurdly wrong, answer. The experimenter found that almost one-third of the subjects changed their minds and accepted the majority's incorrect answer.

The pressure to conform is even stronger among people who are not strangers. During **group-think**, members of a cohesive group endorse a single explanation or answer, usually at the expense of ignoring reality. The group does not tolerate dissenting opinions, seeing them as signs of disloyalty to the group. So members with doubts and alternate ideas do not speak out or contradict the leader of the group, especially when the leader is strong-willed. Group-think decisions often prove disastrous, as when President Kennedy and his top advisors endorsed the CIA's decision to invade Cuba. In short, collective decisions tend to be more effective when members disagree while considering additional possibilities.

Two types of leaders normally emerge from small groups. **Expressive leaders** are *affiliation motivated*. That is, they maintain warm, friendly relationships. They show concern for members' feelings and group cohesion and harmony, and they work to ensure that everyone stays satisfied and happy. Expressive leaders tend to prefer a cooperative style of management. **Instrumental leaders**, on the other hand, are *achievement motivated*. That is, they are interested in achieving goals. These leaders tend to prefer a directive style of management. Hence, they often make good managers because they "get the job done." However, they can annoy and irritate those under their supervision.

Social Organizations

Secondary groups are diverse. Some are large and permanent; others are small and temporary. Some are simple; others are complex. Some have written rules; others do not.

Colleges, businesses, political parties, the military, universities, and hospitals are all examples of **formal organizations**, which are secondary groups that have goal-directed agendas and activities. In contrast to official organizations, the informal relations among workers comprise **informal organizations**. Studies have clearly shown that quality informal relations improve satisfaction on the job and increase workers' productivity. However, professionals seem to place more importance on their relations with their co-workers than blue collar workers do, perhaps because professionals' jobs require more interaction with co-workers.

Goals help to define organizations and what they do, as well as provide standards for measuring efficiency, performance, and success in meeting specific objectives. Whereas most organizations cease to exist if they do not attain their goals, others may thrive because of the continuing need to meet their goals. For example, social service agencies continue to function because they never run out of clients.

Organizations use **rational planning** to achieve their goals. They identify needs, generate alternatives, decide on goals, figure the most effective means to achieve the goals, decide who is best capable of achieving the goals, and then implement a specific plan of action. All of this usually requires strict adherence to policies, which can make large organizations seem businesslike and removed.

Organizational Models

Like groups in general, formal organizations are everywhere. Thus, sociologists have been quite interested in studying how organizations work. To learn more about how organizations operate effectively, sociologists develop **organizational models**. Some models describe the actual characteristics of organizations, while others describe the ideal characteristics for achieving their goals. To date, no single model has adequately described the fully complex nature of organizations in general.

Bureaucratic organizations

Max Weber noted that modern Western society has necessitated a certain type of formal organization: **bureaucracy**. According to Weber, who believed that bureaucracy is the most efficient form of organization possible, the essential characteristics of a bureaucracy include

- Written regulations and rules, which maximize bureaucratic operations and efficiency.

- A highly defined hierarchy of authority, in which those higher in the hierarchy give orders to those lower in the hierarchy. Those who work in bureaucratic settings are called **bureaucrats**.

- Bureaucratic authority resting in various offices or positions, not in individuals.

- Employees being hired based on technical know-how and performance on entry examinations.

- Formal and impersonal record keeping and communications within the organization.

- A paid administrative staff.

Although a bureaucracy itself may be specialized and impersonal, bureaucrats still retain their humanity. Within any bureaucracy, informal relationships invariably form, which can increase worker satisfaction, but only to a point. Informal groups can become disruptive to the efficiency of the bureaucracy.

Critics of Weber note that bureaucracy can also promote inefficiency. A bureaucracy can only formulate rules based on what it knows or expects. Sometimes novel situations or extenuating circumstances arise that the rules do not cover. When the unusual happens, rules may not be of much help.

Collectivist organizations

Unlike Weber, Karl Marx argued that capitalists use bureaucracies to exploit the working class. Marx predicted that bureaucracies would eventually disappear in a communist (classless) society, and that **collectivist organizations**, in which supervisors and workers function as equals for equal wages, would replace the bureaucracies. A variation of the collective organizational model has been tried in China, but with limited success. Critics note that collectivist organizations do not work because "leader" and "followers" inevitably emerge when groups of people are involved.

The Realities of Bureaucracy

Even though many Americans dislike bureaucracy, this organizational model prevails today. Whether or not they wish to admit it, most Americans either work in bureaucratic settings, or at least deal with them daily in schools, hospitals, government, and so forth. Hence, taking a closer look at the pros and cons of bureaucracy is important.

Pros of bureaucracy

Although the vices of bureaucracy are evident (and are discussed in the next section), this form of organization is not totally bad. In other words, benefits to the proverbial "red tape" associated with bureaucracy do exist. For example, bureaucratic regulations and rules help ensure that the Food and Drug Administration (FDA) takes appropriate precautions to safeguard the health of Americans when it is in the process of approving a new medication. And the red tape documents the process so that, if problems arise, data exists for analysis and correction.

Likewise, the impersonality of bureaucracies can have benefits. For example, an applicant must submit a great deal of paperwork to obtain a government student loan. However, this lengthy—and often frustrating—process promotes equal treatment of all applicants, meaning that everyone has a fair chance to gain access to funding. Bureaucracy also discourages favoritism, meaning that in a well-run organization, friendships and political clout should have no effect on access to funding.

Bureaucracies may have positive effects on employees. Whereas the stereotype of bureaucracies is one of suppressed creativity and extinguished imagination, this is not the case. Social research shows that many employees intellectually thrive in bureaucratic environments. According to this research, bureaucrats have higher levels of education, intellectual activity, personal responsibility, self-direction, and open-mindedness, when compared to non-bureaucrats.

Another benefit of bureaucracies for employees is job security, such as a steady salary, and other perks, like insurance, medical and disability coverage, and a retirement pension.

Cons of bureaucracy

Americans rarely have anything good to say about bureaucracies, and their complaints may hold some truth. As noted previously, bureaucratic regulations and rules are not very helpful when unexpected situations arise. Bureaucratic authority is notoriously undemocratic, and blind adherence to rules may inhibit the exact actions necessary to achieve organizational goals.

Concerning this last point, one of bureaucracy's least-appreciated features is its proneness to creating "paper trails" and piles of rules. Governmental bureaucracies are especially known for this. Critics of bureaucracy argue that mountains of paper and rules only slow an organization's capacity to achieve stated goals. They also note that governmental red tape costs taxpayers both time and money.

Parkinson's Law and the Peter Principle have been formulated to explain how bureaucracies become dysfunctional.

Parkinson's Law, named after historian C. Northcote Parkinson, states that work creates more work, usually to the point of filling the time available for its completion. That is, Parkinson believed that bureaucracies always grow—typically 6 percent annually. Managers wish to appear busy, so they increase their workload by creating paper and rules, filling out evaluations and forms, and filing. Then they hire more assistants, who in turn require more managerial time for supervision. Moreover, many bureaucratic budgets rely on the "use it or lose it" principle, meaning the current year's expenditures determines the following year's budget. This provides a deep incentive to spend (even waste) as much money as possible to guarantee an ever-increasing budget. Parkinson's views remain consistent with those of conflict theorists, who hold that bureaucratic growth serves only the managers, who in turn use their increasing power to control the workers.

Approaching bureaucracies from yet another angle, the **Peter Principle**, named after sociologist Laurence Peter, states that employees in a bureaucracy are promoted to the level of their incompetence. In other words, competent managers continually receive promotions until they attain a position in which they are incompetent. And they usually remain in this position until they retire or die. The bureaucracy can only continue because competent employees are constantly working their way up the hierarchical ladder.

Parkinson's Law and the Peter Principle, while fascinating social phenomena, are based on stereotypes and anecdotes rather than on rigorous social science research.

Deviance is any behavior that violates social norms, and is usually of sufficient severity to warrant disapproval from the majority of society. Deviance can be criminal or non-criminal. The sociological discipline that deals with **crime** (behavior that violates laws) is **criminology** (also known as **criminal justice**). Today, Americans consider such activities as alcoholism, excessive gambling, being nude in public places, playing with fire, stealing, lying, refusing to bathe, purchasing the services of prostitutes, and cross-dressing—to name only a few—as deviant. People who engage in deviant behavior are referred to as **deviants**.

The concept of deviance is complex because norms vary considerably across groups, times, and places. In other words, what one group may consider acceptable, another may consider deviant. For example, in some parts of Indonesia, Malaysia, and Muslim Africa, women are circumcised. Termed *clitoridectomy* and *infibulation*, this process involves cutting off a young girl's clitoris and/or sewing shut her labia—usually without any anesthesia. In America, only boys are circumcised; the thought of female circumcision, or *female genital mutilation* as it is known in the United States, is unthinkable.

Theories of Deviance

A number of theories related to deviance and criminology have emerged within the past 50 years or so. Four of the most well-known follow.

Differential-association theory
Edwin Sutherland coined the phrase **differential association** to address the issue of how people *learn* deviance. According to this theory, the environment plays a major role in deciding which norms people learn to violate. Specifically, people within a particular *reference group* provide norms of conformity and deviance, and thus heavily influence the way other people look at the world, including how they react. People also learn their norms from various socializing agents—parents, teachers, ministers, family, friends, co-workers, and the media. In short, people learn criminal behavior, like other behaviors, from their interactions with others, especially in intimate groups.

The differential-association theory applies to many types of deviant behavior. For example, juvenile gangs provide an environment in which young people learn to become criminals. These gangs define themselves as countercultural and glorify violence, retaliation, and crime as means to achieving social status. Gang members learn to be deviant as they embrace and conform to their gang's norms.

Differential-association theory has contributed to the field of criminology in its focus on the developmental nature of criminality. People learn deviance from the people with whom they associate. Critics of the differential-association theory, on the other hand, claim the vagueness of the theory's terminology does not lend itself to social science research methods or empirical validation.

Anomie theory
Anomie refers to the confusion that arises when social norms conflict or don't even exist. In the 1960s, **Robert Merton** used the term to describe the differences between socially accepted goals and the availability of means to achieve those goals. Merton stressed, for instance, that attaining wealth is a major goal of Americans, but not all Americans possess the means to do this, especially members of minority and disadvantaged groups. Those who find the "road to riches" closed to them experience anomie, because an obstacle has

thwarted their pursuit of a socially approved goal. When this happens, these individuals may employ deviant behaviors to attain their goals, retaliate against society, or merely "make a point."

The primary contribution of anomie theory is its ability to explain many forms of deviance. The theory is also sociological in its emphasis on the role of social forces in creating deviance. On the negative side, anomie theory has been criticized for its generality. Critics note the theory's lack of statements concerning the process of learning deviance, including the internal motivators for deviance. Like differential association theory, anomie theory does not lend itself to precise scientific study.

Control theory
According to **Walter Reckless's control theory**, both inner and outer controls work against deviant tendencies. People may want—at least some of the time—to act in deviant ways, but most do not. They have various restraints: *internal controls*, such as conscience, values, integrity, morality, and the desire to be a "good person"; and *outer controls*, such as police, family, friends, and religious authorities. **Travis Hirschi** noted that these inner and outer restraints form a person's **self-control**, which prevents acting against social norms. The key to developing self-control is proper socialization, especially early in childhood. Children who lack this self-control, then, may grow up to commit crimes and other deviant behaviors.

Whereas theory also suggests that people society labels as "criminals" are probably members of subordinate groups, critics argue that this oversimplifies the situation. As examples, they cite wealthy and powerful businesspeople, politicians, and others who commit crimes. Critics also argue that conflict theory does little to explain the causes of deviance. Proponents counter, however, by asserting that the theory does not attempt to delve into etiologies. Instead, the theory does what it claims to do: It discusses the relationships between socialization, social controls, and behavior.

Labeling theory

A type of symbolic interaction, **labeling theory** concerns the meanings people derive from one another's labels, symbols, actions, and reactions. This theory holds that behaviors are deviant only when society labels them as deviant. As such, conforming members of society, who interpret certain behaviors as deviant and then attach this label to individuals, determine the distinction between deviance and non-deviance. Labeling theory questions who applies what label to whom, why they do this, and what happens as a result of this labeling.

Powerful individuals within society—politicians, judges, police officers, medical doctors, and so forth—typically impose the most significant labels. Labeled persons may include drug addicts, alcoholics, criminals, delinquents, prostitutes, sex offenders, retarded people, and psychiatric patients, to mention a few. The consequences of being labeled as deviant can be far-reaching. Social research indicates that those who have negative labels usually have lower self-images, are more likely to reject themselves, and may even act more deviantly as a result of the label. Unfortunately, people who accept the *labeling of others*—be it correct or incorrect—have a difficult time changing their opinions of the labeled person, even in light of evidence to the contrary.

William Chambliss in 1973 conducted a classic study into the effects of labeling. His two groups of white, male, high-school students were both frequently involved in delinquent acts of theft, vandalism, drinking, and truancy. The police never arrested the members of one group, which Chambliss labeled the "Saints," but the police did have frequent run-ins with members of the other group, which he labeled the "Roughnecks." The boys in the Saints came from respectable families, had good reputations and grades in school, and were careful not to get caught when breaking the law. By being polite, cordial, and apologetic whenever confronted by the police, the Saints escaped labeling themselves as "deviants." In contrast, the Roughnecks came from families of lower socioeconomic status, had poor reputations and grades in school, and were not careful about being caught when breaking the law. By being hostile and insolent whenever confronted by the police, the Roughnecks were easily labeled by others and themselves as "deviants." In other words, while both groups committed crimes, the Saints were perceived to be "good" because of their polite behavior (which was attributed to their upper-class backgrounds) and the Roughnecks were seen as "bad" because of their insolent behavior (which was attributed to their lower-class backgrounds). As a result, the police always took action against the Roughnecks, but never against the Saints.

Proponents of labeling theory support the theory's emphasis on the role that the attitudes and reactions of others, not deviant acts *per se*, have on the development of deviance. Critics of labeling theory indicate that the theory only applies to a small number of deviants, because such people are actually caught and labeled as deviants. Critics also argue that the concepts in the theory are unclear and thus difficult to test scientifically.

Crime

Any discussion of deviance remains incomplete without a discussion of **crime**, which is any act that violates written criminal law. Society sees most crimes, such as robbery, assault, battery, rape, murder, burglary, and embezzlement, as deviant. But some crimes, such as those committed in violation of laws against selling merchandise on Sundays, are not deviant at all. Moreover, not all deviant acts are criminal. For example, a person who hears voices that are not there is deviant but not criminal.

A society's criminal justice system punishes crimes. Punishment becomes necessary when criminal acts are so disruptive as to interfere with society's normal functioning.

Limitations of criminal statistics

The FBI's annual *Uniform Crime Report* contains the official crime statistics drawn throughout the United States. Significant biases exist in the reporting and collecting of crime data, and problems occur when people interpret these criminal statistics. Some of these biases include the following:

- Many crimes in the United States go unreported, which makes the validity of crime statistics limited at best.

- Victims are often unwilling to cooperate with authorities.

- Complaints do not always translate into reported crimes. That is, while some victims of crime may complain to police, this does not mean that their complaint ends up reported in the *Uniform Crime Report*.

- Many people do not know how properly to interpret social science statistical data, including criminal statistics. For example, one very common error is attributing cause-and-effect to correlational data. (See Chapter 2.)

- **White-collar crime**, committed by high-status individuals during the course of business, tends not to appear in the *Uniform Crime Report.* Typical white-collar crimes include embezzlement, bribery, criminal price-fixing, insurance fraud, Medicare theft, and so forth.

- Some police and government officials exaggerate or downplay criminal statistics for political purposes. An incumbent politician may report "less crime" statistics in a re-election campaign, while a social service agency may report "more crime" statistics in a proposal for funding.

Types of crime

The types of crimes committed are as varied as the types of criminals who commit them. Most crimes fall into one of two categories— **crimes against people** or **crimes against property**.

Crimes against People

The category of crimes against people includes such crimes as murder, rape, assault, child abuse, and sexual harassment. Violent crimes reported to the police take place on average once every 20 to 30 seconds in the United States. Thus, the chances of being the victim of some form of violent crime in this country are disturbingly high.

Murder or homicide

Most Americans fear murder, which happens to about one in every 10,000 inhabitants. Murders usually occur in the midst of everyday routines and activities. In fact, most murders occur following some degree of social interaction between victim and murderer. Murders generally happen within the context of family or other interpersonal relations, and most victims know their murderer. In some cases, the victim even unintentionally prompts the murderer to attack, by making verbal threats, striking the first blow, or trying to use a weapon, which is called **victim-precipitated murder**. The majority of killers are not psychotic or mentally deranged. While sensational murders and murderers, like the "Son of Sam," receive much publicity, they probably make up a very small percentage of the total.

Studies indicate several interesting facts about murder and murderers:

- Men are much more likely than women to kill and/or be killed.

- Murders are most likely to occur in large urban areas.

- Murders are more common during the months of December, July, and August, and are also more likely to occur on weekend nights and early mornings.

- Alcohol plays a role in nearly two-thirds of all murders.

The question of the role of capital punishment in deterring murder intrigues sociologists and stirs a great deal of debate. The social science literature generally indicates that no relationship exists between capital punishment and homicide rates, although some sociologists may prefer to describe the literature on the topic as inconclusive.

Rape and personal assault

Laws that protect people from unwanted sexual behaviors are appropriate and necessary, and this is certainly the case with **rape**—the forced sexual violation of one person (usually female) by another (usually male). To some, rape is a crime of violence and aggression, not one of sex. To others, it is a crime of both violence and sex.

Rape is hardly a phenomenon of recent origin. Because men have traditionally treated women more like property than as individuals, societies of the past viewed abuses against women less as crimes against them than as crimes against their fathers, husbands, or owners. This thinking has begun to change in recent decades. For instance, some state courts have finally ruled that a woman can charge her husband with *marital rape* if he forces her to have sexual relations.

Although bringing charges against an attacker may now be easier for rape victims, winning a conviction in court is still difficult.

While rape crosses all lines—racial, socioeconomic, age, and marital status—single, white women in their teens and 20s are at the greatest risk of being victims. Most rapists are males between the ages of 18 and 44.

In recent years, the incidence of rape has increased, but authorities believe this is due to more women reporting the crime than to the actual number of rapes increasing. Still, many never report the assault or file charges. Why?

- They may fear being victimized again, this time in the courts.

- They may dread the social stigma of being a rape victim, or the publicity that accompanies a rape report.

- They may realize that the chances of winning a conviction are small.

- They may feel emotionally traumatized and drained.

- They may feel dirty, guilty, and demoralized, coming to the erroneous conclusion that their behavior or dress somehow inadvertently indicated a desire to be forced into sex.

Because of this ambivalence over reporting rape, authorities may never know the exact number of rapes in the United States. One study estimates that between 15 and 25 percent of women in the United States have been or will be victims of rape during their lifetimes. These figures may or may not represent the actual number of rapes taking place in this country, but they are nonetheless alarming.

Six basic types of rape exist: *outsider rape, gang rape, acquaintance rape, date rape, marital rape,* and *statutory rape.* Many people mistakenly believe **outsider rape** (or **stranger rape**), which is an attack from someone entirely unknown to the victim, is the most common type of rape, probably because it is the one victims usually bring to the attention of authorities. Outsider rape is frequently the most violent rape of all. Victims frequently suffer severe and even fatal injury, often through the use of knives, guns, and other weapons. In many cases, perpetrators of outsider rape pick their victims carefully, and plan the best times and places for the assault. **Gang rape** occurs when two or more perpetrators—either strangers or acquaintances—commit rape on the same individual.

The perpetrator of **acquaintance rape** is someone the victim knows. Studies have found acquaintance rape to occur more frequently than any other kind. As many as 95 percent of college female victims may know their attackers. A specific type of acquaintance rape is **date rape**, in which the perpetrator is a dating partner. Date rape can occur at any time during courtship, from the first date to long after a stable relationship has formed. It often happens when one or both individuals have been drinking alcohol or taking drugs, and when one individual takes "no" to sexual pressure from the other to mean "yes" or "maybe."

Some states still do not recognize **marital rape** unless it occurs between separated marital partners or results in serious injury. One research study found that as many as 14 percent of married women report having been raped by their husbands. Although abuse and cruelty are frequent during marital rape, prosecutions are rare.

Marital rape is one aspect of a larger problem—*spouse abuse.* One estimate claims that nearly one million women in the United States each year seek medical treatment for injuries sustained during beatings by their husbands.

Rape is not exclusively a crime committed against women. Men, too, are raped, generally by heterosexual men, but also occasionally by women. Extremely common in prison settings, **male rape** by other males is rarely reported or prosecuted in regular society. Male rape is usually a display of power and dominance over others, such as occurs among prison inmates.

Child abuse
Child abuse is the intentional inflicting of pain, injury, and harm onto a child. Child abuse also includes emotional, psychological, and sexual abuse, including humiliation, embarrassment, rejection, coldness, lack of attention, neglect, isolation, and terrorization.

Adults who were physically and emotionally abused as children frequently suffer from deep feelings of anxiety, shame, guilt, and betrayal. If the experience was especially traumatic and emotionally painful (as it often is), victims may repress memories of the abuse and suffer deep, unexplainable depression as adults. Child abuse almost always interferes with later relationships. Researchers have also noted a wide range of emotional dysfunction both during, soon after, and long after physical abuse, including anxiety attacks, suicidal tendencies, angry outbursts, withdrawal, fear, and depression. Another decidedly negative effect of child abuse, a strong intergenerational pattern, is also worth noting. In other words, many abusers were themselves victims of abuse as children.

In spite of the range and intensity of the after-effects of child abuse, many victims manage to accept the abuse as a regrettable event, but one that they can also leave behind.

One emotionally damaging form of child abuse is **child sexual abuse**. Also known as **child molestation**, child sexual abuse occurs when a teenager or adult entices or forces a child to participate in sexual activity. This activity constitutes perhaps the worst means of exploiting children imaginable. Ranging from simple touching to bodily penetration, child sexual abuse is culturally forbidden in most parts of the world, and is illegal everywhere in the United States. Experts estimate that as many as 25 percent of children in the United States undergo sexual abuse each year. Adults who are sexually attracted to children are known as **pedophiles**.

Every state in the country also has laws against a specific type of child abuse known as **incest**, which is sexual activity between closely related persons of any age. Child sexual abuse is incest when the abuser is a relative, whether or not the relative is blood-related, which explains why stepparents can be arrested for incest when molesting their stepchildren. Not all states have laws forbidding sexual activity among first cousins.

Contrary to popular misconception, incest occurs less frequently than abuse from a person outside the family, such as a family friend, teacher, minister, youth director, or scoutmaster. The perpetrators of incest are typically men; their victims, typically girls in their middle childhood years.

Sexual harassment

Reported more frequently today than ever before, **sexual harassment** is legally defined as unwanted sexual advances, suggestions, comments, or gestures—usually ongoing in nature and involving a supervisor-supervisee relationship (that is, a situation involving unequal power). Sexual harassment takes many forms, such as:

- Verbal harassment or abuse.
- Sexist remarks about a person's body, clothing, or sexual activities.
- Unwanted touching, pinching, or patting.
- Leering or ogling at a person's body.
- Subtle or overt pressure for sexual activity.
- Demanding sexual favors accompanied by implied or overt threats concerning one's job or student status.
- Constant brushing against a person's body.
- Physical assault.

Women are most often the objects of sexual harassment, especially in the workplace. One review of the literature found that 42 percent of women reported having experienced some form of sexual harassment at work, compared to 15 percent of men. The practice is so pervasive in work sites throughout the United States that many women have come to expect it, and the vast majority (over 95 percent) never file a formal complaint. Others simply find another job.

Sexual harassment is not confined to the workplace. For example:

- College students may come under sexual pressure from their instructors, with grades, graduation, and letters of recommendation used as threats or bribes. One survey of university undergraduates found that 29 percent of women and 20 percent of men reported having experienced some form of sexual harassment from instructors.

- Patients of physicians and psychologists may also become the object of unwanted sexual attention from their providers.

- Lawyers may coerce clients into sex in exchange for legal services.

- Even pastors may convince parishioners that sex with the clergy is a viable road to finding spirituality and true peace of mind.

Apparently, no profession, institution, or individual is immune from sexual harassment, as situations of unequal power can exist anywhere. Fortunately, most companies and universities now have policies and reporting structures in place to deal with complaints of sexual harassment, and some states have passed laws prohibiting sexual activity, for example, between therapists and their clients.

The effects of sexual harassment can be numerous and long-lasting. With good jobs at a premium, the possible financial effects of resisting sexual harassment on the job—demotions, pay reductions, and even termination—can be devastating. The psychological effects of sexual pressure on the job, at school, in the doctor's office, or wherever—anxiety, fear, depression, repressed anger, and humiliation—can be equally devastating. Guilt and shame are also common because victims of sexual harassment, similar to victims of rape, may somehow feel responsible. They fear that their dress and/or mannerisms may be bringing on the unwelcome sexual attention.

Crimes against Property

Of the almost 1.5 million Americans under some form of correctional supervision, most are there for offenses against someone else's property. In other words, property crimes are much more common than those against persons are. Property crimes reported to the police take place on average once every 2 to 3 seconds in the United States. Every year about one in 20 Americans falls victim to a property crime.

Computer crime

An emerging type of crime involves using computers to "hack" (break into) military, educational, medical, and business computers. Although software exists to thwart sophisticated hackers, it provides only limited protection for large computer systems. Modest estimates state that *known* computer crimes total some $300 million each year; the amounts could be much higher. Laws dealing with computer crimes are in their infancy.

Victimless crime

In **victimless crime**, all parties consent to the exchange of illegal goods and/or services. In some cases, victims may exist, but not usually. The list of victimless crimes includes illicit drug use, gambling in most areas of the country, the use of illegal sexual materials, public nudity, public drunkenness, vagrancy, loansharking, and prostitution.

A **prostitute** is a person who has sex indiscriminately for pay. Prosecution of prostitutes has been inconsistent, primarily because society has trouble making up its mind about prostitution. The vast majority of Americans disapprove of prostitution—61 percent of males and 83 percent of females believe the practice is "always wrong" or "almost always wrong."

The sheer number of sellers and buyers creates a major problem in trying to arrest and prosecute prostitutes. One conservative estimate says that, at any one time, 5 million American females are engaging in some form of prostitution. Another problem is the criminal justice system's bias toward arresting prostitutes more often than their buyers. Still another is the bureaucratic nature of the criminal justice system, which is excessively time-consuming and expensive. Even if arrested, most prostitutes are poor and cannot afford legal representation, so the system has to cover the costs. The entire ordeal frustrates everyone involved. Rather than attempting to arrest and prosecute prostitutes, some communities prefer to focus their efforts on ridding themselves of overt prostitution, usually by preventing prostitutes from loitering and soliciting in public.

Some prostitutes have organized into active unions with the purpose of promoting prostitutes' civil rights by legalizing or decriminalizing their profession. Some proponents argue that legalizing prostitution would save enforcement dollars, eliminate the need for pimps, bring in license fees and taxes, and keep prostitutes disease-free through regular medical examinations. Others argue that decriminalization would allow people to have control over their work, as well as protect the privacy of prostitutes and their customers.

Organized crime

Organized crime refers to groups and organizations dedicated solely to criminal activity. Historically, leaders of organized crime, or "crime families," have come from different ethnic groups, such as the Italian-American sectors of large U.S. cities.

Organized crime activities are of three basic types:

- Legal activities and businesses, such as restaurants.
- Illegal activities, such as importing and selling narcotics, gambling, and running prostitution rings.
- Racketeering, or the systematic extortion of funds for purposes of "protection."

As one might expect, organized crime can be wildly profitable. Current estimates place organized crime as one of the largest businesses in the United States, even ahead of the automobile industry. Although police and governmental officials continue to fight organized crime, most mobsters have tremendous amounts of money to fight back with high-powered attorneys.

Formal Social Control of Deviance: The Criminal Justice System

Becoming a crime statistic is probably the greatest fear among Americans. To deal with crime and deter criminals, American society makes use of *formal* social controls, particularly the criminal justice system. Sadly, the American criminal justice system is biased. The likelihood of being arrested, convicted, and sentenced appears to be clearly related to finances and social status.

The poor are more likely than the wealthy to be arrested for any category of crime. Why?

- Unlike the wealthy who can commit crimes in the seclusion of their offices or homes, the poor have little privacy. This means the poor are more visible to the police, as well as to other citizens who may complain to law officials.

- Biases in police training and experience may cause police officers to blindly blame crimes on certain groups, such as people of color and lower-class juveniles.

- Finally, the fear of political pressure and "hassles" may prompt law enforcement officers to avoid arresting more affluent and influential members of society.

Poor people typically cannot post bail, so they must wait in jail for their trial. Hence, they are unable to actively work in their own defense. Moreover, when the time for the trial comes, defendants who are not out on bail look guilty because they must enter the courtroom led by police—probably influencing judges and juries. A person who was released on bail enters the courtroom like any other citizen. Social research even indicates that defendants who pay their bail are more likely to be acquitted than those who do not.

Even though the United States entitles all defendants to legal counsel, the quality of this assistance varies. Poor people receive court-appointed lawyers, who may receive lower wages and have a heavy caseload. These lawyers may rush the cases of poor defendants in the interest of time and effort. On the other hand, affluent defendants hire teams of skilled and resourceful lawyers who know how to "work the system."

When it comes to sentencing, the poor generally receive tougher penalties and longer prison terms than do the more affluent convicted of the same crimes. The race of the victims seems to play a role in the harshness of sentencing as well. Regardless of the murderer's race, those murdering whites are more likely to receive the death sentence than those killing minorities.

Nonetheless, the criminal justice system and prison system serve society in several potentially useful ways:

- By being placed in jail, convicted criminals receive "just rewards," or retribution, for their crimes.

- Prisons ideally should deter crimes. As the theory goes, prisons are supposed to keep released criminals from offending again and potential criminals from committing crimes. The social research on this question of deterrence provides mixed results. Prison seems to deter white-collar criminals, for example, but does nothing to deter sex offenders. The literature remains inconclusive with respect to the effects of deterrence on non-criminals.

- Prisons isolate criminals from the general public.

- Prisons ideally serve to rehabilitate criminals into productive citizens who no longer commit crimes. Programs within prisons designed to rehabilitate prisoners include education, personal counseling, and vocational training to prepare them for eventual release and parole.

A short report card on how well prisons achieve their purposes: Prisons successfully punish and isolate inmates, but they seem to be less successful at rehabilitating inmates and deterring future crimes.

Today's prisons are overcrowded, as inmate populations have increased dramatically in recent decades. Excessively brutal conditions cause prisoners to experience a wide variety of health problems, such as heart disease, hypertension, psychological disorders, and suicide. And although incarcerated populations continue to grow, the number of crimes committed in the United States also increases. Sociologists are quick to admit that they have no easy answers that explain the growth in prison populations *and* crimes, or easy solutions (for example, in-home detention, early parole) to change this situation.

Social stratification refers to the unequal distribution around the world of the three Ps: *property*, *power*, and *prestige*. This stratification forms the basis of the divisions of society and categorizations of people. In the case of the latter, **social classes** of people develop, and moving from one stratum to another becomes difficult.

The Basis of Stratification

Normally property (wealth), power (influence), and prestige (status) occur together. That is, people who are wealthy tend also to be powerful and appear prestigious to others. Yet this is not always the case. Plumbers may make more money than do college professors, but holding a professorship is more prestigious than being a "blue collar worker."

The three "Ps" form the basis of social stratification in the United States and around the world, so a detailed discussion of these social "rewards" is in order.

Property
Karl Marx assigned industrial society two major and one minor classifications: the *bourgeoisie* (capitalist class), *petite bourgeoisie* (small capitalist class), and *proletariat* (worker class). Marx made these divisions based on whether the "means of production" such as factories, machines, and tools are owned, and whether workers are hired. **Capitalists** are those who own the methods of production and employ others to work for them. **Workers** are those who do not own the means of production, do not hire others, and thus are forced to work for the capitalists. **Small capitalists** are those who own the means of production but do not employ others. These include self-employed

persons, like doctors, lawyers, and tradesmen. According to Marx, the small capitalists are only a transitional, minor class that is ultimately doomed to becoming members of the proletariat.

Marx held that exploitation is the inevitable outcome of the two major classes attempting to coexist within the same society. In order to survive, workers are coerced into working long, hard hours under less-than-ideal circumstances to maximize the profits of the capitalists. Marx also held that given enough discontent with their exploitation, workers would subsequently organize to revolt against their "employers" to form a "classless" society of economic equals. Marx's predictions of mass revolution never materialized in any highly advanced capitalist society. Instead, the extreme exploitation of workers that Marx saw in the 1860s eventually eased, which resulted in the formation of a large and prosperous white collar population.

Despite Marx's failed predictions, substantial economic inequalities exist today in the United States. **Wealth** refers to the assets and income-producing things that people own: real estate, savings accounts, stocks, bonds, and mutual funds. **Income** refers to the money that people receive over a certain period of time, including salaries and wages. Current social statistics indicate the poorest 20 percent of Americans earn less than 5 percent of the total national income, while the wealthiest 20 percent earn nearly 50 percent of the total. Further, the poorest 20 percent hold far less than 1 percent of the total national wealth, while the wealthiest 20 percent own over 75 percent of the total.

Power

The second basis of social stratification is **power**, or the capacity to influence people and events to obtain wealth and prestige. That is, having power is positively correlated with being rich, as evidenced by the domination of wealthy males in high-ranking governmental positions. Wealthier Americans are also more likely to be politically active as way of ensuring their continued power and wealth. In contrast, poorer Americans are less likely to be politically active, given their sense of powerlessness to influence the process.

Because wealth is distributed unequally, the same is clearly true of power. **Elite theorists** argue that a few hundred individuals hold all of the power in the United States. These **power elite**, who may come from similar backgrounds and have similar interests and values, hold key positions in the highest branches of the government, military, and business world. **Conflict theorists** hold that only a small number of Americans—the capitalists—hold the vast majority of power in the United States. They may not actually hold political office, but they nonetheless influence politics and governmental policies for their own benefit and to protect their interests. An example is the large corporation that tries to limit the amount of fees it must pay through political contributions that ultimately put certain people into office who then sway policy decisions.

On the other hand, **pluralist theorists** hold that power is not in the hands of the elite or a few, but rather it is widely distributed among assorted competing and diverse groups. In other words, unlike elitists and Marxists, pluralists note little if any inequality in the distribution of power. For instance, citizens can influence political outcomes by voting candidates into or out of office. And the power of labor groups is balanced by the power of businesses, which is balanced by the power of the government. In a democracy, no one is completely powerless.

Prestige

A final basis of social stratification is the unequal distribution of **prestige**, or an individual's status among his or her peers and in society. Although property and power are objective, prestige is subjective, for it depends on other people's perceptions and attitudes. And while prestige is not as tangible as money and influence, most Americans want to increase their status and honor as seen by others.

Occupation is one means by which prestige can be obtained. In studies of occupational prestige, Americans tend to answer consistently— even across the 1970s, 1980s, and 1990s. For example, being a physician ranks among the highest on the scale, whereas being a shoe shiner ranks near the bottom.

The way people rank professions appears to have much to do with the level of education and income of the respective professions. To become a physician requires much more extensive training than is required to become a cashier. Physicians also make a great deal more money than cashiers, ensuring their higher prestige ranking.

To occupation must be added social statuses based on race, gender, and age. Even though being a professor is highly ranked, also being a racial minority and a female may negatively affect prestige. As a result, individuals who experience such **status inconsistency** may suffer from significant anxiety, depression, and resentment.

Types of Social Classes of People

Social class refers to a group of people with similar levels of wealth, influence, and status. Sociologists typically use three methods to determine social class:

- The **objective method** measures and analyzes "hard" facts.

- The **subjective method** asks people what they think of themselves.

- The **reputational method** asks what people think of others.

Results from these three research methods suggests that in the United States today approximately 15 to 20 percent are in the poor, lower class; 30 to 40 percent are in the working class; 40 to 50 percent are in the middle class; and 1 to 3 percent are in the rich, upper class.

The lower class

The lower class is typified by poverty, homelessness, and unemployment. People of this class, few of whom have finished high school, suffer from lack of medical care, adequate housing and food, decent clothing, safety, and vocational training. The media often stigmatize the lower class as "the underclass," inaccurately characterizing poor people as welfare mothers who abuse the system by having more and more babies, welfare fathers who are able to work but do not, drug abusers, criminals, and societal "trash."

The working class

The working class are those minimally educated people who engage in "manual labor" with little or no prestige. Unskilled workers in the class—dishwashers, cashiers, maids, and waitresses—usually are underpaid and have no opportunity for career advancement. They are often called the **working poor**. Skilled workers in this class—carpenters, plumbers, and electricians—are often called **blue collar workers**. They may make more money than workers in the middle class—secretaries, teachers, and computer technicians; however, their jobs are usually more physically taxing, and in some cases quite dangerous.

The middle class

The middle class are the "sandwich" class. These **white collar workers** have more money than those below them on the "social ladder," but less than those above them. They divide into two levels according to wealth, education, and prestige. The **lower middle class** is often made up of less educated people with lower incomes, such as managers, small business owners, teachers, and secretaries. The **upper middle class** is often made up of highly educated business and professional people with high incomes, such as doctors, lawyers, stockbrokers, and CEOs.

The upper class

Comprising only 1 to 3 percent of the United States population, the upper class holds more than 25 percent of the nation's wealth. This class divides into two groups: *lower-upper* and *upper-upper*. The

lower-upper class includes those with "new money," or money made from investments, business ventures, and so forth. The **upper-upper class** includes those aristocratic and "high-society" families with "old money" who have been rich for generations. These extremely wealthy people live off the income from their inherited riches. The upper-upper class is more prestigious than the lower-upper class.

Wherever their money comes from, both segments of the upper class are exceptionally rich. Both groups have more money than they could possibly spend, which leaves them with much leisure time for cultivating a variety of interests. They live in exclusive neighborhoods, gather at expensive social clubs, and send their children to the finest schools. As might be expected, they also exercise a great deal of influence and power both nationally and globally.

Social Mobility

When studying social classes, the question naturally arises: Is it possible for people to move within a society's stratification system? In other words, is there some possibility of **social mobility**, or progression from one social level to another? *Yes*, but the degree to which this is possible varies considerably from society to society.

On the one hand, in a closed society with a **caste system**, mobility can be difficult or impossible. Social position in a caste system is decided by assignment rather than attainment. This means people are either born into or marry within their family's caste; changing caste systems is very rare. An example of the rigid segregation of caste systems occurs today in India, where people born into the lowest caste (the "untouchables") and can never become members of a higher caste. South Africa also has a caste system.

On the other hand, in an open society with a **class system**, mobility is possible. The positions in this stratification system depend more on achieved status, like education, than on ascribed status, like gender.

For example, the United States' social stratification is of this type, meaning movement between social strata is easier and occurs more frequently.

Patterns of social mobility

Several patterns of social mobility are possible:

- **Horizontal mobility** involves moving within the same status category. An example of this is a nurse who leaves one hospital to take a position as a nurse at another hospital.

- **Vertical mobility**, in contrast, involves moving from one social level to another. A promotion in rank in the Army is an example of **upward mobility**, while a demotion in rank is **downward mobility**.

- **Intragenerational mobility**, also termed **career mobility**, refers to a change in an individual's social standing, especially in the workforce, such as occurs when an individual works his way up the corporate ladder.

- **Intergenerational mobility** refers to a change in social standing across generations, such as occurs when a person from a lower-class family graduates from medical school.

Sociologists in the United States have been particularly interested in this latter form of mobility, as it seems to characterize the "American Dream" of opportunity and "rags to riches" possibilities.

Structural mobility and individual mobility

Major upheavals and changes in society can enhance large numbers of people's opportunities to move up the social ladder at the same time. This form of mobility is termed **structural mobility**. Industrialization, increases in education, and postindustrial computerization have allowed large groups of Americans since 1900 to improve their social status and find higher-level jobs than did their parents. Nevertheless, not everyone moves into higher-status positions. Individual characteristics—such as race, ethnicity, gender, religion, level of education, occupation, place of residence, health, and so on—determine **individual mobility**. In the United States, being a member of a racial minority, female, or a disabled person have traditionally limited the opportunities for upward mobility.

Poverty

Any discussion of social class and mobility would be incomplete without a discussion of **poverty**, which is defined as the lack of the minimum food and shelter necessary for maintaining life. More specifically, this condition is known as **absolute poverty**. Today it is estimated that more than 35 million Americans—approximately 14 percent of the population—live in poverty. Of course, like all other social science statistics, these are not without controversy. Other estimates of poverty in the United States range from 10 percent to 21 percent, depending on one's political leanings. This is why many sociologists prefer a *relative,* rather than an *absolute*, definition of poverty. According to the definition of **relative poverty**, the poor are those who lack what is needed by most Americans to live decently because they earn less than half of the nation's median income. By this standard, around 20 percent of Americans live in poverty, and this has been the case for at least the past 40 years. Of these 20 percent, 60 percent are from the working class poor.

Causes of poverty

Poverty is an exceptionally complicated social phenomenon, and trying to discover its causes is equally complicated. The stereotypic (and simplistic) explanation persists—that the poor cause their own poverty—based on the notion that anything is possible in America. Some theorists have accused the poor of having little concern for the future and preferring to "live for the moment"; others have accused them of engaging in self-defeating behavior. Still other theorists have characterized the poor as fatalists, resigning themselves to a **culture of poverty** in which nothing can be done to change their economic outcomes. In this culture of poverty—which passes from generation to generation—the poor feel negative, inferior, passive, hopeless, and powerless.

The "blame the poor" perspective is stereotypic and not applicable to all of the underclass. Not only are most poor people able and willing to work hard, they do so when given the chance. The real trouble has to do with such problems as minimum wages and lack of access to the education necessary for obtaining a better-paying job.

More recently, sociologists have focused on other theories of poverty. One theory of poverty has to do with the flight of the middle class, including employers, from the cities and into the suburbs. This has limited the opportunities for the inner-city poor to find adequate jobs. According to another theory, the poor would rather receive welfare payments than work in demeaning positions as maids or in fast-food restaurants. As a result of this view, the welfare system has come under increasing attack in recent years.

Again, no simple explanations for or solutions to the problem of poverty exist. Although varying theories abound, sociologists will continue to pay attention to this issue in the years to come.

The effects of poverty
The effects of poverty are serious. Children who grow up in poverty suffer more persistent, frequent, and severe health problems than do children who grow up under better financial circumstances.

- Many infants born into poverty have a low birth weight, which is associated with many preventable mental and physical disabilities. Not only are these poor infants more likely to be irritable or sickly, they are also more likely to die before their first birthday.

■ Children raised in poverty tend to miss school more often because of illness. These children also have a much higher rate of accidents than do other children, and they are twice as likely to have impaired vision and hearing, iron deficiency anemia, and higher than normal levels of lead in the blood, which can impair brain function.

Levels of stress in the family have also been shown to correlate with economic circumstances. Studies during economic recessions indicate that job loss and subsequent poverty are associated with violence in families, including child and elder abuse. Poor families experience much more stress than middle-class families. Besides financial uncertainty, these families are more likely to be exposed to series of negative events and "bad luck," including illness, depression, eviction, job loss, criminal victimization, and family death. Parents who experience hard economic times may become excessively punitive and erratic, issuing demands backed by insults, threats, and corporal punishment.

Homelessness, or extreme poverty, carries with it a particularly strong set of risks for families, especially children. Compared to children living in poverty but having homes, homeless children are less likely to receive proper nutrition and immunization. Hence, they experience more health problems. Homeless women experience higher rates of low-birth-weight babies, miscarriages, and infant mortality, probably due to not having access to adequate prenatal care for their babies. Homeless families experience even greater life stress than other families, including increased disruption in work, school, family relationships, and friendships.

Sociologists have been particularly concerned about the effects of poverty on the "black underclass," the increasing numbers of jobless, welfare-dependent African Americans trapped in inner-city ghettos. Many of the industries (textiles, auto, steel) that previously offered employment to the black working class have shut down, while newer industries have relocated to the suburbs. Because most urban jobs either require advanced education or pay minimum wage, unemployment rates for inner-city blacks are high.

Even though Hispanic Americans are almost as likely as African Americans to live in poverty, fewer inner-city Hispanic neighborhoods have undergone the same massive changes as many black neighborhoods have. Middle and working class Hispanic families have not left their *barrio,* or urban Spanish-speaking neighborhood, in large numbers, so most Hispanic cultural and social institutions there remain intact. In addition, local Hispanic-owned businesses and low-skill industries support the barrio with wage-based, not welfare-based, businesses.

Climbing out of poverty is difficult for anyone, perhaps because, at its worst, poverty can become a self-perpetuating cycle. Children of poverty are at an extreme disadvantage in the job market; in turn, the lack of good jobs ensures continued poverty. The cycle ends up repeating itself until the pattern is somehow broken.

Feminist perspective on poverty
Finally, recent decades have witnessed the **feminization of poverty**, or the significant increase in the numbers of single women in poverty alone, primarily as single mothers. In the last three decades the proportion of poor families headed by women has grown to more than 50 percent. This feminization of poverty has affected African-American women more than any other group.

This feminization of poverty may be related to numerous changes in contemporary America. Increases in unwanted births, separations, and divorces have forced growing numbers of women to head poor households. Meanwhile, increases in divorced fathers avoiding child support coupled with reductions in welfare support have forced many of these women-headed households to join the ranks of the underclass. Further, because wives generally live longer than their husbands, growing numbers of elderly women must live in poverty.

Feminists also attribute the feminization of poverty to women's vulnerability brought about by the patriarchal, sexist, and gender-biased nature of Western society, which does not value protecting women's rights and wealth.

The term **race** refers to groups of people who have differences and similarities in biological traits deemed by society to be **socially significant**, meaning that people treat other people differently because of them. For instance, while differences and similarities in eye color have not been treated as socially significant, differences and similarities in skin color have.

Although some scholars have attempted to establish dozens of racial groupings for the peoples of the world, others have suggested four or five. An example of a *racial category* is *Asian,* (or *Mongoloid*), with its associated facial, hair color, and body type features. Yet too many exceptions to this sort of racial grouping have been found to make any racial categorizations truly viable. This fact has led many sociologists to indicate that no clear-cut races exist—only assorted physical and genetic variations across human individuals and groups.

Certainly, obvious physical differences—some of which are inherited—exist between humans. But how these variations form the basis for social prejudice and discrimination has nothing to do with genetics but rather with a social phenomenon related to outward appearances. **Racism**, then, is prejudice based on socially significant physical features. A **racist** believes that certain people are superior, or inferior, to others in light of racial differences. Racists approve of **segregation**, or the social and physical separation of classes of people.

Ethnicity refers to shared cultural practices, perspectives, and distinctions that set apart one group of people from another. That is, ethnicity is a shared cultural heritage. The most common characteristics distinguishing various ethnic groups are ancestry, a sense of history, language, religion, and forms of dress. Ethnic differences are not inherited; they are *learned.*

Most countries today consist of different ethnic groups. Ideally, countries strive for **pluralism**, where people of all ethnicities and races remain distinct but have social equality. As an example, the United States is exceptionally diverse, with people representing groups from all over the globe, but lacking in true pluralism. The same can be said of the ethic diversity of the former Soviet Union with its more than 100 ethnic groups, some having more than a million members.

Minorities

Racial and ethnic groups whose members are especially disadvantaged in a given society may be referred to as **minorities**. This term has more to do with social factors than with numbers. For example, while people with green eyes may be in the minority, they are not considered to be "true" minorities. From a sociological perspective, minorities generally have a sense of *group identity* ("belonging together") and *separateness* ("being isolated from others"). They are also *disadvantaged* in some way when compared to the majority of the population. Of course, not all minorities experience all three of these characteristics; some people are able to transcend their **master status**, or social identity as defined by their race or ethnicity.

Most minority groups are locked in to their minority standing, regardless of their achieved level of personal success. They live in certain regions of a country, certain cities, and certain neighborhoods—the poorest areas, more often than not. That is, ethnicity is often associated with social inequalities of power, prestige, and wealth—all of which can lead to hostility between groups within a society. Finally, to preserve their cultural identity, most minorities value **endogamy**, or marriage within the group. Put another way, intermarriage between minority and majority groups, or even between different minority groups, is not always sanctioned by both groups. Prohibiting intermarriage reduces the possibility of **assimilation**, or gradual adoption of the dominant culture's patterns and practices.

Prejudice and Discrimination

Prejudice and discrimination have been prevalent throughout human history. **Prejudice** has to do with the inflexible and irrational attitudes and opinions held by members of one group about another, while **discrimination** refers to behaviors directed against another group. Being prejudiced usually means having preconceived beliefs about groups of people or cultural practices. Prejudices can either be positive or negative — both forms are usually preconceived and difficult to alter. The negative form of prejudice can lead to discrimination, although it is possible to be prejudiced and not act upon the attitudes. Those who practice discrimination do so to protect opportunities for themselves by denying access to those whom they believe do not deserve the same treatment as everyone else.

It is unfortunate that prejudices against racial and ethnic minorities exit, and continue to flourish, despite the "informed" modern mind. One well-known example of discrimination based on prejudice involves the Jews, who have endured mistreatment and persecution for thousands of years. The largest scale attempt to destroy this group of people occurred during World War II, when millions of Jews were exterminated in German concentration camps in the name of Nazi ideals of "racial purity." The story of the attempted **genocide**, or systematic killing, of the Jews—as well as many other examples of discrimination and oppression throughout human history—has led sociologists to examine and comment upon issues of race and ethnicity.

The sources of prejudice
Sociologists and psychologists hold that some of the emotionality in prejudice stems from subconscious attitudes that cause a person to ward off feelings of inadequacy by projecting them onto a target group. By using certain people as **scapegoats**—those without power who are unfairly blamed—anxiety and uncertainty are reduced by attributing complex problems to a simple cause: "Those people are the source of all my problems." Social research across the globe has

shown that prejudice is fundamentally related to low self-esteem. By hating certain groups (in this case, minorities), people are able to enhance their sense of self-worth and importance.

Social scientists have also identified some common social factors that may contribute to the presence of prejudice and discrimination:

1. *Socialization.* Many prejudices seem to be passed along from parents to children. The media—including television, movies, and advertising—also perpetuate demeaning images and stereotypes about assorted groups, such as ethnic minorities, women, gays and lesbians, the disabled, and the elderly.

2. *Conforming behaviors.* Prejudices may bring support from significant others, so rejecting prejudices may lead to losing social support. The pressures to conform to the views of families, friends, and associates can be formidable.

3. *Economic benefits.* Social studies have confirmed that prejudice especially rises when groups are in direct competition for jobs. This may help to explain why prejudice increases dramatically during times of economic and social stress.

4. *Authoritarian personality.* In response to early socialization, some people are especially prone to stereotypical thinking and projection based on unconscious fears. People with an **authoritarian personality** rigidly conform, submit without question to their superiors, reject those they consider to be inferiors, and express intolerant sexual and religious opinions. The authoritarian personality may have its roots in parents who are unloving and aloof disciplinarians. The child then learns to control his or her anxieties via rigid attitudes.

5. *Ethnocentrism.* **Ethnocentrism** is the tendency to evaluate others' cultures by one's own cultural norms and values. It also includes a suspicion of outsiders. Most cultures have their ethnocentric tendencies, which usually involve stereotypical thinking.

6. *Group closure*. **Group closure** is the process whereby groups keep clear boundaries between themselves and others. Refusing to marry outside an ethnic group is an example of how group closure is accomplished.

7. *Conflict theory*. Under **conflict theory**, in order to hold onto their distinctive social status, power, and possessions, privileged groups are invested in seeing that no competition for resources arises from minority groups. The powerful may even be ready to resort to extreme acts of violence against others to protect their interests. As a result, members of underprivileged groups may retaliate with violence in an attempt to improve their circumstances.

Solutions to prejudice

For decades, sociologists have looked to ways of reducing and eliminating conflicts and prejudices between groups:

- One theory, the **self-esteem hypothesis**, is that when people have an appropriate education and higher self-esteem, their prejudices will go away.

- Another theory is the **contact hypothesis**, which states that the best answer to prejudice is to bring together members of different groups so they can learn to appreciate their common experiences and backgrounds.

- A third theory, the **cooperation hypothesis**, holds that conflicting groups need to cooperate by laying aside their individual interests and learning to work together for shared goals.

- A fourth theory, the **legal hypothesis**, is that prejudice can be eliminated by enforcing laws against discriminative behavior.

To date, solutions to prejudice that emphasize change at the individual level have not been successful. In contrast, research sadly shows that even unprejudiced people can, under specific conditions of war or economic competition, become highly prejudiced against their perceived "enemies." Neither have attempts at desegregation in schools been successful. Instead, many integrated schools have witnessed the formation of ethnic cliques and gangs that battle other groups to defend their own identities.

Changes in the law have helped to alter some prejudiced attitudes. Without changes in the law, women might never have been allowed to vote, attend graduate school, or own property. And racial integration of public facilities in America might never have occurred. Still, laws do not necessarily change people's attitudes. In some cases, new laws can increase antagonism toward minority groups.

Finally, **cooperative learning**, or learning that involves collaborative interactions between students, while surely of positive value to students, does not assure reduction of hostility between conflicting groups. Cooperation is usually too limited and too brief to surmount all the influences in a person's life.

To conclude, most single efforts to eliminate prejudice are too simplistic to deal with such a complex phenomenon. Researchers, then, have focused on more holistic methods of reducing ethnocentrism and cultural conflicts. They have noted that certain conditions must be met before race relations will ever improve:

- A desire to become better acquainted.
- A desire to cooperate.
- Equal economic standing and social status.
- Equal support from society.

Sociologists speculate that one reason prejudice is still around is the fact that these conditions rarely coincide.

Ethnic and Racial Minorities in the United States

Although Americans have traditionally hailed their country as the "land of opportunity," this has been truer for some groups than for others. Following are brief overviews of four minority groups in the United States: Native Americans, African Americans, Hispanic Americans, and Asian Americans.

Native Americans

Native Americans, or "American Indians," settled in North America long before any Europeans arrived. Yet they have now lived as foreigners and forgotten members of their own land for more than 200 years. In the 1800s, they were corralled onto "reservations" where they had few opportunities for growing food, hunting animals, or obtaining work. Only in this decade has the Native-American population grown to more than 2 million. Most live on reservations or in rural areas primarily located in the Western states. In recent decades, though, there has been an influx of Native Americans into urban areas.

American Indians are the poorest ethnic group in America. The vast majority live in substandard housing, and about 30 percent live in utter poverty, meaning they are very prone to malnutrition and diseases. The average Native American attends school less than 10 years, and the drop-out rate is double the national average. The rate of Indian unemployment is as high as 80 percent in some parts of the country. Further complicating these matters is the fact that the rate of alcoholism for Native Americans is more than five times that of other Americans.

Native Americans remain a tightly knit and culturally minded people. Neither urban nor rural Indians have necessarily lost their original tribal identities. For instance, the Navajo—who have the most populated and largest reservation in this country—have held fast to their cultural patterns, even though many Navajo have worked in industrial cities.

Inspired in part by the civil rights movement, Native Americans have become politically active in recent years. The American Indian Movement (AIM) is one example of how Indians from various tribes have organized to preserve their authentic culture, prevent further violations of their territorial rights, and pursue other legal matters. Although some goals have been attained, the small number of Native Americans in the United States limits their lobbying power and legal pull.

African Americans

Perhaps more than that of any other minority, the history of African Americans in this country has been a long and complex story. During the slave trade in the early history of the United States, millions of blacks were brought from Africa. By the late 1700s, almost 4 million slaves lived in the southern states. While some slave masters may have tried to treat their black slaves humanely, the slaves felt deeply their loss of homeland, family, and freedom. In addition, harsh working conditions, physical beatings, manacles, branding, and castration were common. Nor did the slaves always passively give in to their masters' whims; sometimes slaves rebelled against their masters. Out of all of this oppression evolved a variety of uniquely African-American forms of art and music, including gospel, jazz, and the blues.

The formal abolition of slavery during the Civil War forever altered the life of blacks, especially in the South. Yet the one form of group closure—slavery—was replaced by another—discrimination. The behavior of the former slaves was closely monitored, and they were quickly punished for their "transgressions." The result was continual denial of black people's political and civil rights. Legislation was also passed legalizing segregation of blacks from whites in public places like trains and restaurants. However, following the Civil War, most states in the South passed legislation against the interests of blacks, which became known as the **Jim Crow laws**. The laws, for example, prohibited blacks from attending white schools, theaters, restaurants, and hotels.

During the early decades of the 20th century, thousands of southern blacks moved to the North because of increased job opportunities. However, this migration did not always set well with northerners. Race riots exploded, and blacks encountered numerous forms of discrimination in housing, work, and politics.

This migration north continued both during and after World War II, especially with the increased automation being used on southern plantations. But blacks migrating north after World War II soon found the opportunities for work slim. Increased automation coupled with unions that exerted control over many occupations added to the prejudice and discrimination experienced by blacks.

The Civil Rights Movement
Blacks were largely denied opportunities for education and personal advancement until the early 1950s and 1960s. It was only then that the National Urban League and the National Association for the Advancement of Colored People (NAACP) began to have an effect on black civil rights.

Even before World War II, social advocates began challenging segregation in the military, as well as on buses and in schools, restaurants, swimming pools, and other public places. In 1954, in *Brown v. Board of Education of Topeka, Kansas,* the Supreme Court declared that "separate educational facilities are inherently unequal"—a decision that formed the basis of the civil rights movement of the 1950s to the 1970s. The decision was strongly opposed in some states, and groups like the Ku Klux Klan (KKK), which had formed during reconstruction, organized to intimidate and persecute blacks.

In 1955 in Montgomery, Alabama, a 42-year-old African-American woman—Rosa Parks—refused to surrender her seat on a bus so that white people could sit. She was subsequently arrested, which spawned mass demonstrations and bus boycotts. Eventually, a Baptist minister, **Martin Luther King, Jr.**, organized and led marches and campaigns of nonviolent resistance to discrimination. But responses to the movement were far from nonviolent. As examples, the National Guard would prohibit black students from entering public facilities, and police would disperse protesters with clubs, fire hoses, and attack dogs. Still, the demonstrations continued until, in 1964, Congress passed a Civil Rights bill banning discrimination in education, employment, public facilities, and in governmental agencies. Additional bills in later years were passed to outlaw discrimination in housing and to ensure the rights of blacks to vote. As might be expected, a great deal of resistance arose to the implementation of the new laws protecting blacks' civil rights. Civil rights leaders were threatened, beaten up, and even killed—as was the case of Martin Luther King, Jr., in 1968. During the remainder of the 1960s, major race riots broke out in cities across the nation.

Affirmative action

The 1960s and 1970s witnessed the beginnings of **affirmative action**, or action taken to provide equal opportunity, to end discrimination. Most instances of affirmative action have proven to be controversial. An example is forced school busing, in which children were taken by bus to schools outside their normal school districts in an attempt to force integration in school systems. Other examples of affirmative action attempted in the 1970s and 1980s included having "quotas" (percentages of represented groups) employed in public agencies and colleges. Critics of affirmative action argued that the resulting "reverse discrimination," or action taken to provide opportunity only to underrepresented groups, was not a cure for social ills. Fixed quotas were finally declared illegal.

Blacks today

Sociologists debate the actual effects of the civil rights movement. Although the movement seems to have had some impact, the degree to which that impact has caused lasting social change remains in question.

The unemployment rate of blacks compared to whites is the same as it was in the early 1960s. Employment opportunities for black men have worsened, and a greater percentage of black men have given up on the work force. Likewise, little seems to have improved in terms of neighborhood segregation. Research has reaffirmed that blacks continue to be victims of discrimination in the real estate market.

On a more positive note, black and white children now attend the same schools, and black and white students attend the same colleges. Some urban schools and colleges, however, have larger numbers of black students because of the movement of whites to suburban and rural areas.

Blacks have also made some gains in elective politics; the number of black public officials has increased dramatically since the 1960s. Yet these changes are still relatively minor, as blacks make up only a few percentage points of the one-half million elected public offices in the United States.

Hispanic Americans

The modern United States includes those areas annexed in 1848 as a result of the American war with Mexico. The descendants of those Mexican people, as well those of other culturally Spanish countries, are referred to as *Hispanics* or *Latinos*. Four primary groups of Hispanics exists in the United States today: Mexican Americans, Puerto Ricans, Cubans, and smaller Spanish-speaking groups from Central and South

America. Whether due to large waves of immigrations since the 1960s or the tendency to have large families, the Hispanic population in this country is increasing at a remarkable rate. The Hispanic population may overtake the black population within the next few decades.

Mexican Americans

Although Mexican Americans live throughout the United States, the largest numbers tend to be concentrated in the Southwest. Although most Mexican Americans live in cities, they generally live in *barrios,* which are Spanish-speaking neighborhoods. Some 20 percent live in poverty, and most work in menial jobs. Because many speak only minimal English, they can expect few educational and job opportunities. Some Mexican Americans have resisted assimilating into the dominant English-speaking culture, instead preferring to preserve their own cultural identity.

Illegal immigration of workers from Mexico has been a problem for some time. Wages and benefits are significantly better in the United States, which prompts some despcrate families—however great the risks involved—to attempt to enter the United States illegally in the hopes of securing an adequate future. Large numbers of these Mexicans are intercepted and sent back each year by immigration officials, but most simply try again. Illegal immigrants, who are usually willing to perform jobs that others will not, are employable at much cheaper wages than American workers. This leads to a variety of social and political issues for Americans, including increased welfare costs and discrimination.

Puerto Ricans

Puerto Ricans have been American citizens since the early 1900s, when Puerto Rico became a self-governing Commonwealth of the United States. Because Puerto Rico is a poor island, many of its residents have immigrated to the mainland to improve their circumstances. Puerto Ricans have tended to settle in New York City, where nearly half continue to live below the line of poverty. This has resulted in a *reverse migration* of Puerto Ricans back to their island in the hopes of finding a better life.

Puerto Rican activists continue to argue over the destiny of Puerto Rico. Today, Puerto Rico is not a full state within the United States; it is a **commonwealth**, or self-governing political entity that maintains a voluntary relationship with a larger nation. Whether Puerto Rico will become the 51st state of the United States, continue as a Commonwealth, or seek independence remains to be seen.

Cubans
More than half a million Cubans left their home following Fidel Castro's rise to power in 1959. Unlike other Hispanic immigrants, most of these settled in Florida and came from professional and white-collar backgrounds. These early Cuban Americans have thrived in the United States, many in comparable positions to those they left in Cuba. In the 1980s another wave of Cuban immigration occurred, although these people tended to come from poorer conditions. Unlike their predecessors, these later Cuban immigrants have been on par with other Hispanic communities in this country. Both groups of Cuban immigrants are primarily political refugees.

Asian Americans

About 5 million Americans are of Asian heritage, the majority being Chinese, Japanese, and Filipino. Other Asian Americans include people from Korea, Vietnam, Pakistan, and India.

Most Japanese and Chinese workers were brought into the United States by their employers beginning in the late 1800s. Japanese immigrants tended to settle in Pacific states, especially California. In one of America's darker moments, following the Japanese attack on Pearl

Harbor during World War II, all Japanese-American citizens were forced to report to "relocation centers," which were nothing more than concentration camps. After the war, these Japanese Americans integrated into larger American society rather than returning to segregated neighborhoods. Over the years, this minority group has rivaled the education and income levels of whites.

Chinese immigrants also settled in California and worked in such industries as railroad construction and mining. Working- and lower-class whites viewed these immigrants as a potential threat to their jobs, and so began an intense campaign of prejudice and discrimination against these people. The Chinese responded by forming distinct cultural neighborhoods, or "Chinatowns," where they had a fighting chance to protect themselves from white aggression.

The Immigration Act of 1965 brought about increased immigration of Asians into the United States. Immigrant Chinese Americans now tend to avoid the "Chinatowns" of the native-born Chinese Americans. Many of these foreign-born Chinese work in menial occupations, but ever-growing numbers are working in professional positions. Today, Chinese Americans continue to integrate into mainstream society, where they often work, live, and socialize alongside whites and other groups.

According to traditional American norms, males and females of every age are *supposed* to play out their respective culturally defined masculine and feminine roles. But sociologists know that a fallacy exists here. Believing that one *must* live out a certain predetermined gender role is one of those "rules" of life that many follow, but few understand. Just because a society defines what behaviors, thoughts, and feelings are appropriately "masculine" and "feminine" does not mean that these role definitions are necessarily desirable. Hence, sociologists are especially interested in the effects that gender and society have on each other.

Definitions

Gender refers to an individual's anatomical sex, or **sexual assignment**, and the cultural and social aspects of being male or female.

An individual's personal sense of maleness or femaleness is his or her **gender identity**.

Outward expression of gender identity according to cultural and social expectations is a **gender role**. Either gender can live out a gender role (for example, being a homemaker) but not a **sex role**, which is anatomically limited to one gender (gestating and giving birth being limited to females, for example).

An individual's **sexual orientation** refers to her or his relative attraction to members of the same sex (*homosexual*), other sex (*heterosexual*), or both sexes (*bisexual*).

All of these—gender, sexual assignment, gender identity, gender role, sex role, and sexual orientation—form an individual's **sexual identity**.

Gender Identity

Sociologists are particularly interested in gender identity and how (or if) it determines gender roles. Gender identity appears to form very early in life and is most likely irreversible by age 4. Although the exact causes of gender identity remain unknown, biological, psychological, and social variables clearly influence the process. Genetics, prenatal and postnatal hormones, differences in the brain and the reproductive organs, and socialization all interact to mold a person's gender identity.

Biological influences on gender identity

Sexual differentiation, which encompasses the physiological processes whereby females become females and males become males, begins prenatally. The differences brought about by physiological processes ultimately interact with social-learning influences **postpartum** (after birth) to establish firmly a person's gender identity.

Genetics is the scientific study of heredity. Geneticists study **genes**, the basic units of heredity that determine inherited characteristics. Genes are composed of deoxyribonucleic acid (DNA). Three primary patterns of genetic transmission are **dominant** (expressed trait that is visibly apparent), **recessive** (unexpressed trait that is not visibly apparent), and **sex-linked** inheritance (trait carried on one of the sex chromosomes, usually X).

Determination of an embryo's chromosomal sex is genetic, occurring at conception. This process involves **chromosomes**, which are the biological structures containing biological "blueprints," or **genes**. The egg, or **ovum**, always carries an X chromosome, and the sperm carries either a Y or an X chromosome. A **zygote** is the product of conception: a fertilized egg. A male zygote (XY) is the product of the fusion of an egg with a sperm carrying a Y chromosome; a female zygote (XX), the product of the fusion of an egg with a sperm carrying an X chromosome. The X chromosome provides valuable genetic material essential to life and health. The Y chromosome is smaller than the X, and carries little more than directions for producing a male.

Psychological and social influences on gender identity
Gender identity is ultimately derived from both chromosomal makeup and physical appearance, but this does not mean that psychosocial influences are missing. **Socialization**, or the process whereby a child learns the norms and roles that society has created for his or her gender, plays a significant role in the establishment of her or his sense of femaleness or maleness. If a child learns she is a female and is raised as a female, the child believes she is female; if told he is a male and raised as a male, the child believes he is male.

Beginning at birth, most parents treat their children according to the child's gender as determined by the appearance of their genitals. Parents even handle their baby girls less aggressively than their baby boys. Children quickly develop a clear understanding that they are either female or male, as well as a strong desire to adopt gender-appropriate mannerisms and behaviors. This normally occurs within two years, according to many authorities. In short, biology "sets the stage," but children's interactions with the social environment actually determine the nature of gender identity.

Some people are unable to merge the biological, psychological, and social sides of their gender. They suffer **gender dysphoria**, or emotional confusion and pain over their gender identity. Specifically, some believe they were born into the wrong-gender body, that their internal sense of gender is inconsistent with their external sexual biology. This condition is termed **transsexualism**. Transsexuals may desire to be rid of their primary and secondary sexual structures and acquire those of the other sex by undergoing **sex-reassignment surgery**. Transsexuals should not be confused with **transvestites**, who enjoy wearing the clothing of the other gender.

Gender Roles

Gender roles are cultural and personal. They determine how males and females should think, speak, dress, and interact within the context of society. Learning plays a role in this process of shaping gender roles. These **gender schemas** are deeply embedded cognitive frameworks regarding what defines masculine and feminine. While various **socializing agents**—parents, teachers, peers, movies, television, music, books, and religion—teach and reinforce gender roles throughout the lifespan, parents probably exert the greatest influence, especially on their very young offspring.

As mentioned previously, sociologists know that adults perceive and treat female and male infants differently. Parents probably do this in response to their having been recipients of gender expectations as young children. Traditionally, fathers teach boys how to fix and build things; mothers teach girls how to cook, sew, and keep house. Children then receive parental approval when they conform to gender expectations and adopt culturally accepted and conventional roles. All of this is reinforced by additional socializing agents, such as the media. In other words, learning gender roles always occurs within a social context, the values of the parents and society being passed along to the children of successive generations.

Gender roles adopted during childhood normally continue into adulthood. At home, people have certain presumptions about decision-making, child-rearing practices, financial responsibilities, and so forth. At work, people also have presumptions about power, the division of labor, and organizational structures. None of this is meant to imply that gender roles, in and of themselves, are good or bad; they merely exist. Gender roles are realities in almost everyone's life.

Gender Stereotypes

Gender stereotypes are simplistic generalizations about the gender attributes, differences, and roles of individuals and/or groups. Stereotypes can be positive or negative, but they rarely communicate accurate information about others. When people automatically apply gender assumptions to others regardless of evidence to the contrary, they are perpetuating gender stereotyping. Many people recognize the dangers of gender stereotyping, yet continue to make these types of generalizations.

Traditionally, the **female stereotypic role** is to marry and have children. She is also to put her family's welfare before her own; be loving, compassionate, caring, nurturing, and sympathetic; and find time to be sexy and feel beautiful. The **male stereotypic role** is to be the financial provider. He is also to be assertive, competitive, independent, courageous, and career-focused; hold his emotions in check; and always initiate sex. These sorts of stereotypes can prove harmful; they can stifle individual expression and creativity, as well as hinder personal and professional growth.

The weight of scientific evidence demonstrates that children learn gender stereotypes from adults. As with gender roles, socializing agents—parents, teachers, peers, religious leaders, and the media—pass along gender stereotypes from one generation to the next.

One approach to reexamining conventional gender roles and stereotypes is **androgyny**, which is the blending of feminine and masculine attributes in the same individual. The **androgyne**, or androgynous person, does not neatly fit into a female or male gender role; she or he can comfortably express the qualities of both genders. Parents and other socializing agents can teach their children to be androgynous, just as they can teach them to be gender-biased.

Emerging as a powerful sociopolitical force beginning in the 1960s, the **feminist movement**, or **women's liberation movement**, has lobbied for the rights of women and minorities. Feminists have fought hard to challenge and redefine traditional stereotypic gender roles.

Social Stratification and Gender

Throughout most of recorded history and around the globe, women have taken a "back seat" to men. Generally speaking, men have had, and continue to have, more physical and social power and status than women, especially in the public arena. Men tend to be more aggressive and violent then women, so they fight wars. Likewise, boys are often required to attain proof of masculinity through strenuous effort. This leads to males holding public office, creating laws and rules, defining society, and—some feminists might add—controlling women. For instance, not until this century were women in the United States allowed to own property, vote, testify in court, or serve on a jury. Male dominance in a society is termed **patriarchy**.

Whereas in recent decades major strides toward gender equality have been made, sociologists are quick to point out that much remains to be done if inequalities in the United States are ever to be eliminated. Behind much of the inequalities seen in education, the workplace, and politics is **sexism**, or prejudice and discrimination because of gender. Fundamental to sexism is the assumption that men are superior to women.

Sexism has always had negative consequences for women. It has caused some women to avoid pursuing successful careers typically described as "masculine"—perhaps to avoid the social impression that they are less desirable as spouses or mothers, or even less "feminine."

Sexism has also caused women to feel inferior to men, or to rate themselves negatively. In **Philip Goldberg's** classic 1968 study, the researcher asked female college students to rate scholarly articles that were allegedly written by either "John T. McKay" or "Joan T. McKay." Although all the women read the same articles, those who thought the author was male rated the articles higher than the women who thought the author was female. Other researchers have found that men's resumes tend to be rated higher than women's. More recently, though, researchers have found the gap in these sorts of ratings to be closing. This may be due to social commentary in the media regarding sexism; growing numbers of successful women in the workforce, or discussion of Goldberg's findings in classrooms.

In short, sexism produces inequality between the genders—particularly in the form of discrimination. In comparable positions in the workplace, for example, women generally receive lower wages than men. But sexism can also encourage inequality in more subtle ways. By making women feel inferior to men, society comes to accept this as the truth. When that happens, women enter "the race" with lower self-esteem and fewer expectations, often resulting in lower achievements.

Sexism has brought gender inequalities to women in many arenas of life. But inequality has been a special problem in the areas of higher education, work, and politics.

Sexism in Higher Education

Only in recent years have women been able to take advantage of opportunities to receive **higher education**, that is, to earn a college or university degree. Although some exceptions exist, women were generally barred from universities and colleges, especially professional and graduate programs, until the 1960s. In fact, the more prestigious the program, the more gender discrimination women encountered. The women's movement was largely responsible for pressuring the government to pass laws making sex discrimination illegal in educational settings. **Title IX** requires schools to eliminate gender discrimination in admissions and financial aid policies, gender-segregated classes and sports programs, and administrative, faculty, and staff hiring practices.

Today, women are more likely than men to attend college and earn a first or second degree, usually in a liberal arts area that does not lead to a high-paying job. But women are less likely than men to receive advanced degrees.

Sexism occurs in the administration and on the faculties of institutions of higher learning. Research has consistently demonstrated that, compared with men, women are less likely to be hired, be promoted, or receive tenure. Women also make less money than men, even though women academicians teach as well as men, conduct research, and generate grants.

Sexism in the Workplace

Sexism in education is clearly associated with sexism in the workplace. When women are expected to "stay in the home," they are unable to access the necessary educational resources to compete with men in the job market. If by chance they are able to secure a position, women may be less prepared educationally for the task, and thus draw lower wages.

In recent decades more women have entered the United States workforce. After WWII (from about 1947), about 30 percent of women were employed outside the home; today, at the start of the 21st century, the figure is well over 50 percent. (Some estimates approach 75 percent if "part-time" jobs are included.) Yet women are far from treated equally on the job. Typically, they hold lower-paying, lower-status jobs than men. In fact, women may account for only 25 percent of the upper-level managers in large corporations. And although half of the employees in the largest, most prestigious firms around the United States may be women, perhaps as few as 5 percent or less actually hold senior positions.

In general, women are under-represented in the higher-status, higher-paying occupations, such as university teaching, law, engineering, and medicine. In contrast, women are over-represented in the lower-paying occupations, such as public-school teaching, nursing, and secretarial work. In stereotypical female jobs, referred to as **women's ghettos**, women are subordinate to the positions of men. For example, executives supervise secretaries who are likely to be women, and lawyers supervise paralegals, who are also likely to be women.

Women in the same jobs as men usually earn less, even though these women may have the same or better training, education, and skills. As a general statistic, women make only 60 percent or less than men in comparable positions. Why this disparity? Sociologists speculate that, in some cases, the fact that women often must take time off to have and raise children interrupts their career path. As much as Americans may hate to admit it, women in the United States still bear the primary responsibilities of child-rearing. Conflicting demands may partly explain why married women with children are more likely to leave their jobs than are childless and single women. Also, men are seen as the "chief bread winners," so the belief is that they should be paid more than women in order to support their families. Whatever the reason, paying women less than men for equally demanding work is discrimination.

A related issue, sexual harassment in the workplace, is discussed in more detail in Chapter 6.

Sexism in Politics

With female voters outnumbering male voters (more than 50 percent of voters are women), one might think that women could easily take over in political arenas. However, sociologists note that many women have hesitated to enter the world of politics, believing it to be too corrupt or a "good old boy" activity. Also, women who enter political office must contend with "dammed-if-you-do-or-don't" standards. Women politicians may be viewed as inattentive wives and mothers. If women are avid family members, then they are viewed as inattentive public servants. Men politicians, on the other hand, do not normally have to confront such double standards.

Although men still control political parties, a growing number of women are attaining high political offices. Still, women hold only about 5 percent of all political offices, so the situation is far from balanced. Since the 1990s, increasing numbers of women have entered the political races for the Senate, House, and the office of State Governor. Today, women are more encouraged to enter a race as large numbers of male incumbents leave office. They may be more likely to win for reasons of public credibility, especially when they run against politicians who are lacking in integrity. Women also tend to attract voters who also support issues like child welfare, national health care, protection of the environment, and abortion rights.

Perhaps more importantly, though, women have been exercising more and more political clout as voters. Beginning in the 1980s, the percentages of voting women have surpassed those of men. Because women tend to vote for more liberal candidates who support social programs than do men, they have the potential to heavily influence the outcomes of elections.

In short, women are making strides, but also have a long way to go before reaching equality with men in the world of politics.

Gender and Homosexuality

Related to the topic gender is **sexual orientation**, or a person's sexual, romantic, affectionate, and emotional attraction to members of the same sex, the opposite sex, or both. A person who is attracted to members of the opposite sex is **heterosexual**, or "straight." A person who is attracted to members of the same sex is **homosexual**, or "gay" (male) or "lesbian" (female). A person who is attracted to members of both sexes is **bisexual**, or "bi."

Most sociologists today refer to *sexual orientation* rather than *sexual preference*. The latter implies that sexual attraction is a choice, which many researchers believe is not the case.

In the 1940s and 1950s, **Alfred Kinsey** and his associates discovered that sexual orientation exists along a continuum. Prior to Kinsey's research into the sexual habits of Americans, experts generally believed that most individuals were either heterosexual or homosexual. Kinsey speculated that the categories of sexual orientation were not so distinct. On his surveys, many Americans reported having had at least minimal attraction to members of the same gender, although most had never acted act on this attraction. In short, Kinsey and colleagues brought to the attention of medical science the notion of heterosexuality, homosexuality, and bisexuality all being separate but related sexual orientations.

Prevalence of Homosexuality and Bisexuality

Because many people are hesitant to answer sexual surveys, obtaining exact percentages on the prevalence of homosexuality is difficult. Further complicating matters is that perhaps as few as 10 percent of the homosexuals in the United States have actually *come out of the closet* (admitted to being gay) to family and friends. The rest who "stay in the closet" are **passing** ("passing themselves off" as heterosexual). Support groups and National Coming Out Day (celebrated annually on October 11) are available for gays and lesbians who wish to tell their families and friends about their sexual orientation.

Today's estimates are that as many as 4 percent of men and 1 to 2 percent of women in the United States are homosexual. The Centers for Disease Control further estimates that approximately 2.5 million U.S. men are exclusively homosexual (or 1 percent of the total U.S. population, currently at 250 million), with an additional 2.5 to 7.5 million men engaging in occasional homosexual relations.

Regarding such "occasional" relations, Kinsey found that roughly 37 percent of men and 13 percent of women surveyed reported having had at least one same-sex encounter. In another study in 1989, **R. E. Fay** found that about 20 percent of nearly 1,200 men surveyed reported having had at least one same-sex experience, and that about 3 percent reported having such contacts either "fairly often" or "occasionally." Interestingly, 8 percent of married men in this same study also reported having homosexual contacts either "fairly often" or "occasionally."

Social scientists generally agree that the popular figure of "10 percent" of the population as homosexual is probably an overestimate. Estimates of homosexuality, however, in certain settings like prisons will be higher because of **situational homosexuality**, or homosexual behavior in the absence of opposite-sex partners.

Information on bisexuality is even less available because so many researchers define bisexuality as a type of homosexuality. Self-labeling is another issue. Some who have both opposite-sex and same-sex relations consider themselves heterosexual, while others who marry and raise children as a social "cover" consider themselves gay, and not bisexual.

Many bisexuals disagree with the notion that bisexuality is "the best of both worlds." As a group, bisexuals often feel alienated from both homosexuals and heterosexuals. Bisexual communities, support groups, and resources are available, but they are few in comparison to the resources available for homosexuals. No doubt, this population will become increasingly visible in the future as more people become comfortable with "coming out."

Social Stratification and Homosexuality

Gays and lesbians, especially in the last 20 years, have actively sought to end what they perceive as prejudice and discrimination against them based on their sexual orientation. They have worked at all levels of society to change laws, fight job discrimination and harassment, eliminate homophobia and gay bashing (that is, violence directed toward homosexuals), lobby for funding to fight the AIDS virus, and educate the public about homosexuality and homosexuals. Although many gays and lesbians believe they have come a long way toward achieving their goals, others believe they still have much work to do before achieving true "gay liberation."

The **gay rights movement**, as it is popularly known today, came into full swing with the 1969 Stonewall riot. The New York police had a long history of targeting patrons of gay bars for harassment and arrests. In June 1969, they raided the Stonewall Inn, a gay bar in New York's Greenwich Village. When the patrons of the bar resisted, a riot followed that lasted into the next day. The incident prompted the formation of numerous gay rights groups and the organization of marches, demonstrations, and yearly commemorative parades and activities, including the Gay Pride March.

Many people incorrectly assume that the gay rights movement began with the Stonewall riot, when in fact more than 40 gay and lesbian organizations were already in place at that time. Two of the more visible groups in the 1950s and 1960s were the Mattachine Society and the Daughters of Bilitis. After the Stonewall riot, gays and lesbians organized into such political groups and service agencies as Act Up, the Gay Liberation Front, Gay Activists Alliance, Gay and Lesbian Advocates and Defenders, Lesbian Rights Project, National Gay and Lesbian Task Force, National Gay Rights Advocates, and Queer Nation, to name only a few.

Finally, on the topic of gay and lesbian political activism, Warren Blumenfeld and Diane Raymond in their 1993 book *Looking at Gay and Lesbian Life* (published by Beacon Press) noted that being politically active is risky, and people with few or compromised rights frequently cannot afford to take risks. Nevertheless, to define activism more broadly, any open affirmation of homosexuality in a predominantly heterosexual society is a political act. And the variety of openly lesbian and gay organizations, political groups, and service agencies in existence demonstrates the movement's success, as well as the development of a sense of identity and community, a "consciousness of kind," that has grown out of this movement, dramatically improving the quality of life.

The **economy** is a social system that produces, distributes, and consumes goods and services in a society. Three sectors make up an economy: primary, secondary, and tertiary.

- The **primary sector** refers to the part of the economy that produces raw materials, such as crude oil, timber, grain, or cotton.

- The **secondary sector**, made up of mills and factories, turns the raw materials into manufactured goods, like fuel, lumber, flour, or fabric.

- The **tertiary sector** refers to services rather than goods, and includes distribution of manufactured goods, food and hospitality services, banking, sales, and professional services like architects, physicians, and attorneys.

These three sectors do not exist equally in an economy and have changed considerably throughout the history of humanity.

Historical Overview of Economics

As Chapter 3 explains, humans first relied upon hunting and gathering to survive. Social systems of subsistence depended upon the family or small groups for food and did not have a recognizable economy. But through agriculture, specialization, settlement, and trade, an economy did emerge.

With the development of agriculture came pastoral and horticultural societies with more dependable food supplies and surplus. This surplus allowed division of labor, and many in the society took on new roles—specializing in making clothes, tools, or shelter. People could settle in one place and begin producing a surplus of other goods, which in turn led to trade. The primary sector dominated this pre-industrial economy, and cottages or homes produced limited manufacturing. Sociologists studying the transformation from hunting and gathering to pre-industrial society primarily interest themselves in how surplus, trade, and accumulation of possessions led to social inequality (the situation where some people have more possessions and power than others).

Primary sector dominance shifted to the secondary sector in the mid-eighteenth century with the Industrial Revolution. Beginning in England with the invention of steam power, the force of production moved from muscle to machine. The limited manufacturing in cottages or homes of pre-industrial society gave way to centralized, mass production in factories. Workers, now earning wages, became more specialized, doing single repetitive tasks rather than making a product from start to finish.

The secondary sector dominance gave way to tertiary sector dominance in many economies during the mid-twentieth century. Economists call such economies **postindustrial** because they depend upon service industries and high technology. As the steam engine powered the Industrial Revolution, computers have fueled the Information Revolution in the twentieth century. In the **Information Revolution**, information and ideas have replaced manufactured goods as the basis for the economy. Consequently, the economy requires a more literate labor force, which must now communicate through computers rather than simply manipulating machines.

Today, countries may be agricultural (primary sector), industrial (secondary sector), or postindustrial (tertiary sector). The poorest countries are agricultural, while the wealthiest are postindustrial. With the rise of technology, computers, and the Internet, sociologists and economists point to the growing **global economy** (an economy where product or information development, production, and distribution cross national borders). For example, automobiles, a major production of industrialized nations, were once manufactured and assembled in one country. With the global economy, other countries make many parts for vehicles considered "American," and workers in the United States now assemble vehicles once considered "foreign."

Predominant Economic Systems

The two predominant economic systems today are capitalism and socialism. Between these two opposite extremes lies a continuum of variations on the models.

Capitalism

Three key principles define the economic system of capitalism:

- Private ownership of production and distribution of goods and services

- Competition, or the laws of supply and demand directing the economy

- Profit-seeking, or selling goods and services for more than their cost of production

Laissez-faire (French for "hands off") capitalism represents a pure form of capitalism not practiced by any nation today. The ideology driving today's capitalism says that competition is in the best interest of consumers. Companies in competition for profit will make better products cheaper and faster to gain a larger share of the market. In this system, the market—what people buy and the laws of supply and demand—dictates what companies make, and how much of it they make. Workers are motivated to work harder so they can afford more of the products they want.

Supporters of a capitalist system point to the higher production, greater wealth, and higher standard of living displayed by capitalist countries such as the United States. Critics, however, charge that while the standard of living may be higher, greater social inequity remains. They also denounce greed, exploitation, and high concentration of wealth and power held by a few.

Socialism

Three key principles also define the economic system of socialism:

- State ownership of production and distribution of goods and services

- Central economy

- Production without profit

The ideology of socialism directly rejects the ideology of capitalism. In a socialist economic system, the state determines what to produce and at what price to sell it. Socialism eliminates competition and profit, and focuses upon social equality—supplying people with what they need, whether or not they can pay. The ideals driving socialism come from Karl Marx who saw all profit as money taken away from workers. He reasoned that the labor used to produce a product determined the value of that product. The only way for a company to arrive at profit is to pay workers less than the value of the product. Thus, wherever profit exists, workers are not receiving the true value of their labor.

Just as nations do not adhere to pure capitalism, neither do nations adhere to pure socialism. In pure socialism, all workers would earn exactly the same wage. Most Socialist countries do pay managers and professionals such as doctors a higher wage. But, because the state employs all members of the society, thereby controlling the wages, far less disparity exists between highest and lowest wage earners.

Supporters of socialism, then, point to its success at achieving social equality and full employment. Critics counter that with central planning's gross inefficiency, the economy cannot produce wealth and all people are poorer. They also object to what they see as unnecessary control of personal lives and limited rights—exploitation.

Democratic socialism and state capitalism

Ironically, critics of both capitalism and socialism accuse each system of exploitation. Consequently, some nations have carved out systems more in the middle of the continuum between the two.

One hybrid is **democratic socialism**, which is an economic system where the government maintains strict economic controls while maintaining personal freedom. Scandinavian nations, Canada, England, and Italy all practice democratic socialism. Sweden provides the most common example in which high taxation provides extensive social programs.

State capitalism is another economic hybrid. In this economic system, large corporations work closely with the government, and the government protects their interests with import restrictions, investment capital, and other assistance. This economic system commonly exists in Asian countries such as Japan and South Korea.

Modern Corporations and Multinationals

A **corporation** is a business that is legally independent from its members. Corporations may incur or pay debt, negotiate contracts, sue and be sued. Corporations range in size from local retail stores to Ford Motor Company or General Electric, the nation's largest corporation. These larger corporations sell stocks to shareholders, and the shareholders legally own the company. Management of the company remains separate from, but accountable to, the ownership. The shareholders are organized with a board of directors who hold regular meetings and make decisions on broad policies governing the corporation. Although many Americans own stock, they normally do not participate in regular board meetings or exert significant control over corporate decisions.

Sometimes corporations with closely related business may share board members, which is called an **interlocking directorate**. In this arrangement a manufacturer, a financial services company, and an insurance company with shared business also share the same board members. These few individuals, then, exert power over multiple companies whose business is interdependent.

A **conglomerate** is a corporation made up of many smaller companies, or subsidiaries, that may or may not have related business interests. The buying and selling of corporations for profit—rather than for the service or products they provide—form conglomerates. The process of corporate merger often leads to large layoffs because, as companies combine forces, many jobs are duplicated in the other company. For example, a conglomerate may take over a smaller company, including that company's marketing department. The conglomerate will already have a marketing department capable of handling most of the new acquisition's needs. Therefore, as many as half or all of the acquired marketing department employees would lose their jobs. The same situation often occurs when two corporations of a similar size merge.

Other types of corporations include *monopolies*, *oligopolies*, and *multinationals*. **Monopolies** occur when a single company accounts for all or nearly all sales of a product or service in a market. Monopolies are illegal in the United States because they eliminate competition and can fix prices, which hurts consumers. In other words, monopolies interfere with capitalism. The U.S. government does consider some monopolies legal, however, such as utilities

where competition would be difficult to implement without distressing other social systems. But even utility monopolies have seen increased competition in recent years. Telephone companies were the first utility to witness a rise in competition with the breakup of AT&T in the 1980's. Recently electric power companies have seen deregulation and increased competition in some regions as well.

Oligopolies exist when several corporations have a monopoly in a market. The classic example of an oligopoly would be American auto makers until the 1980s. Ford, Chrysler, and General Motors manufactured nearly all vehicles built in America. As globalization has increased, so has competition, and few oligopolies exist today.

Multinationals are corporations that conduct business in many different countries. These corporations produce more goods and wealth than many smaller countries. Their existence, though, remains controversial. They garner success by entering less-developed nations, bringing industry into these markets with cheaper labor, and then exporting those goods to more-developed countries. Business advocates point to the higher standard of living in most countries where multinationals have entered the economy. Critics charge that multinationals exploit poor workers and natural resources, creating environmental havoc.

Labor Unions

In the face of large corporations, individual workers have typically felt alienated and vulnerable. While corporations may not hear the individual, laborers recognized that they would hear a united voice. This realization led the workers to develop **labor unions**—organized groups of laborers who advocate improved conditions and benefits for workers. Labor unions remained strong throughout much of the early and mid-twentieth century. In recent years, however, labor unions in the United States have lost numbers and power. With increasing globalization, corporate mergers, and downsizing, many experts expect to see an increase in labor unions again as workers seek stability and a greater share in the benefits of the global economy.

Politics and the Major Forms of Political Structure

Politics is the social structure and methods used to manage a government or state. Just as varying types of economic theories and systems exist, many varying political theories and systems exist as well.

The political system in use depends upon the nation-state. A **nation** is a people with common customs, origin, history, or language. A **state**, on the other hand, is a political entity with legitimate claim to monopolize use of force through police, military, and so forth. The term **nation-state** refers to a political entity with the legitimate claim to monopolize use of force over a people with common customs, origin, history, or language. Sociologists and political scientists prefer the term nation-state to "country" because it is more precise.

While many different political structures have existed throughout history, three major forms exist in modern nation-states: totalitarianism, authoritarianism, and democracy.

Totalitarianism

Totalitarianism is a political system that exercises near complete control over its citizens' lives and tolerates no opposition. Information is restricted or denied by complete control of mass media, close monitoring of citizens and visitors, and forbidding the gathering of groups for political purposes opposed to the state. Constant political propaganda, such as signs, posters, and media that focus the populace on the virtues of the government, characterizes these nation states. Obviously, some totalitarian governments maintain more extreme laws than others do. Totalitarian nation-states include North Korea, Chile, many African and Middle Eastern nations, Vietnam, and others.

Authoritarianism

Authoritarianism is a political system less controlling than totalitarianism, but still denying citizens the right to participate in government. A dictatorship, in which the primary authority rests in one individual, represents one type of authoritarian government. Dictators rule China, Cuba, Ethiopia, Haiti, and many African nations. In these systems, strong militaries and political parties support the dictators. Another form of authoritarianism is a monarchy, in which the primary authority rests in a family and is passed down through generations. In the past, most monarchies exerted near absolute power—in Saudi Arabia the ruling family still does. Most remaining monarchies today, however, such as those in the Scandinavian nations, Great Britain, Denmark, and the Netherlands, are **constitutional monarchies** where the royal families serve only as symbolic heads of state. Parliament or some form of democratic electoral process truly governs these nation states.

Democracy

Democracy is a political system where the government is ruled either directly by the people or through elected officials who represent them. Most democracies today rely upon a system of representatives to make decisions. The most common examples of democracies are the United States, Canada, Germany, and many other European nations.

Politics in the United States

The election of public officials and the balance of power between the three branches of government (executive, legislative, and judicial) carry out democracy in the United States. This system, which makes each branch accountable to the others, restricts the authority of any one branch of the government.

The legislative branch, or Congress (comprised of the House of Representatives and the Senate), writes, amends, and passes bills, which the President, as head of the executive branch, must then sign into law.

The executive branch through the President may veto any bill. If the President does veto a bill, the legislative branch may overturn this action with a two-thirds majority in both legislative houses.

The judicial branch, or Supreme Court, may overturn any law passed by the legislature and signed by the President.

The people elect the executive and legislative branches, while the executive branch appoints the members of the judicial branch, subject to approval by the legislature.

The most prominent election in the United States is that of President. While many people mistakenly believe that the popular vote or the Congress directly elects the President, the Electoral College (whose vote is dictated by the popular vote) officially elects the President. To maintain a balance of power, states elect the legislature separately. Each state elects two representatives to the Senate for six years; only a portion of the Senate seats come up for election every two years. States have a varying number of congressional seats based on population. Thus, for example, California elects more representatives than other Western states because it has a higher population. Population is constitutionally determined through a 10-year national census.

The President appoints the U.S. Supreme Court (the nine-member judicial branch), but both branches of the legislature must approve the President's choices. This appointment is for life to remove the justice system from short-term political influence.

The two-party system

Two predominant political parties comprise the United States government—Republicans and Democrats:

- **Republicans** generally espouse more conservative (or "right") views and support policies to reduce federal regulations, strengthen the military, and boost capitalist endeavors.

- **Democrats**, on the other hand, generally lean toward more liberal (or "left") opinions and support policies to strengthen social services, protect the environment, and make businesses accountable to labor.

Although the parties possess different philosophical stances, a continuum exists between them. The United States system is unlike most democracies, which have more than two parties. In multi-party systems, political groups with specialized agendas (such as labor, business, and environment) represent their interests. With the more generalized American system, the two parties must appeal to a broader range of people to be elected. Therefore, both parties work to appear "centrist"—that is, neither too liberal nor too conservative. In this system, third party candidates face great difficulty getting elected. In fact, third-party candidates have only found success at the state and local level. The last time voters elected a third-party president was in 1860 when Abraham Lincoln became President. Yet third-party candidates have begun to influence present-day elections and may prompt an eventual restructuring of the two traditional political parties.

Lobbyists and Political Action Committees (PACs)

Without specific representation in multiple political parties, special
interest groups must find alternative methods of getting their voices
heard in the legislative process. Many companies and other groups
hire professional lobbyists to advocate for their causes.

A **lobbyist** is someone paid to influence government agencies,
legislators, and legislation to the best interests of their clients.
Lobbyists may even write the legislation that the legislator presents
to a committee or the legislature. Lobbyists represent nearly all industries and interests, including insurance, auto manufacturing, tobacco,
environment, women, minorities, education, technology, textiles,
farming, and many others. Lobbyists, who are usually lawyers, are
often former members of the legislature or have held other government positions. Companies and interest groups hire them because of
their influence and access from their former jobs. For example, after
spending decades as a Senator from Oregon and leaving office in dis-
grace over misconduct, Bob Packwood returned to Washington, D.C.
as a paid lobbyist for business interests in the Pacific Northwest.

Political Action Committees, or **PACs**, are special interest
groups that raise money to support and influence specific candidates
or political parties. These groups may take an interest in economic or
social issues, and include groups as diverse as the American Medical
Association, the Trial Lawyers Association, the National Education
Association, and the National Rifle Association. In recent years these
groups have proved to be powerful and wealthy forces in elections.
They often possess more money than the candidates and can run
advertising campaigns that support or oppose the viewpoints or
actions of a candidate running for office. They may also heavily influence state or local campaigns for ballot measures. PACs bear much
of the responsibility for drastic increases in campaign spending in
recent years. Many groups and officials are now calling for restrictions on such spending to limit PAC influence and maintain a balance
of power among all interested constituencies.

The Pluralist and Power-Elite Models of politics
Sociologists recognize two main models when analyzing political structures, particularly in the United States:

- The **Pluralist Model** argues that power is dispersed throughout many competing interest groups and that politics is about negotiation. One gains success in this model through forging alliances, and no one group always gets its own way.

- The **Power-Elite Model** argues the reverse, claiming that power rests in the hands of the wealthy—particularly business, government, and the military. These theorists claim that, because power is so heavily concentrated in a few at the top, the average person cannot be heard. In addition, they say that the competitors who are claimed to work as balances simply do not exist.

Experts examining these diverse viewpoints recognize substantial research to support both views.

Education generally refers to a social institution responsible for providing knowledge, skills, values, and norms.

The Development and Function of Universal Education

Universal education in the United States grew out of the political and economic needs of a diverse and fledgling nation. Immigrants came from many cultures and religious beliefs; consequently, no common national culture existed. Without a cohesive structure to pass on the democratic values that had brought the country's independence, the new nation risked fragmentation.

Founding Father Thomas Jefferson and dictionary-compiler Noah Webster recognized in the 1800s that democracy depended upon a well-educated, voting populace able to reason and engage in public debate. The nation did not fully realize their vision of education immediately. Many states saw "the nation" as a conglomeration of nation states. This fragmented political atmosphere created an education system with no system at all: Each locality administered its own system with no connection to any other locality. To complicate matters, public schools at that time required tuition, making them inaccessible to the poor, unless the poor were fortunate enough to attend for free. Many religious groups opened parochial schools, but, again, only the rich could afford to attend. Only the wealthiest could afford high school and college. Furthermore, while the political structure may have required an educated voter, the economic structure, which was still based on agriculture (see Chapter 10), did not require an educated worker.

Horace Mann and tax-supported education

The fact that average citizens could not afford to send their children to school outraged **Horace Mann**, a Massachusetts educator now called the "father of American education." To solve this problem, in 1837 he proposed that taxes be used to support schools and that the Massachusetts government establish schools throughout the state. These "common schools" proved such a success that the idea spread rapidly to other states. Mann's idea coincided with a nation about to undergo industrialization and increasing demands from labor unions to educate their children. The Industrial Revolution generated a need for a more specialized, educated work force. It also created more jobs, which brought more immigrants. Political leaders feared that too many competing values would dilute democratic values and undermine stability, so they looked to universal education as a means of Americanizing immigrants into their new country.

As the need for a specialized, educated workforce continued to increase, so did education and its availability. This led to **compulsory education**; all states had mandates by 1918 that all children must attend school through the eighth grade or age 16. High school was optional, and society considered those with an eighth-grade education fully educated. As of 1930, less than 20 percent of the population graduated from high school; by 1990 more than 20 percent graduated from college.

The rise of the credential society

The need for a specialized workforce has increased exponentially over the decades. Today, Americans live in a **credential society** (one that depends upon degrees and diplomas to determine eligibility for work). Employers, predominantly in urban areas, who must draw from a pool of anonymous applicants need a mechanism to sort out who is capable of work and who is not. Those who have completed a college degree have demonstrated responsibility, consistency, and presumably, basic skills. For many positions, companies can build upon the basic college degree with specific job training. Some professions require highly specialized training that employers cannot accommodate, however. Lawyers, physicians, engineers, computer technicians, and, increasingly, mechanics must complete certified programs—often with lengthy internships—to prove their competency.

The demand for credentials has become so great that it is changing the face of higher education. Many students who attend college for a year or two (or even complete a two-year Associate's Degree), and then enter the workforce in an entry-level job, may find themselves needing a four-year degree. They discover that while employers hire those without four-year degrees, advancement in the company depends upon the credential of a Bachelor's degree. Oftentimes, regardless of their years of experience or competence on the job, employees who have the appropriate credentials receive advancement. Once again, economics changes education. Most employees with families and full-time employment cannot afford to quit work or work part-time and attend college.

Many colleges have responded with **alternative educational delivery systems** for those who are employed full time. For example:

- At some colleges, students with a minimum number of credits may apply for accelerated degree programs offered in the evenings or on Saturdays.

- Some colleges allow students to attend courses one night per week for 18 to 24 months and complete all the course work needed for a specific four-year degree, such as Business Administration.

This demand for credentialed employees combined with new educational opportunities such as internet courses, video classes, and home study has changed the demographics of colleges that offer these programs. In some cases, nontraditional students, or adult learners, comprise as many as half of the students attending a college.

Theories of Education

Historically, American education served both political and economic needs, which dictated the function of education. Today, sociologists and educators debate the function of education. Three main theories represent their views: the functionalist theory, the conflict theory, and the symbolic interactionist theory.

The functionalist theory

The **functionalist theory** focuses on the ways that universal education serves the needs of society. Functionalists first see education in its manifest role: conveying basic knowledge and skills to the next generation. **Durkheim** (the founder of functionalist theory; see Chapter 1) identified the latent role of education as one of socializing people into society's mainstream. This "moral education," as he called it, helped form a more-cohesive social structure by bringing together people from diverse backgrounds, which echoes the historical concern of "Americanizing" immigrants.

Functionalists point to other latent roles of education such as transmission of **core values** and social control. The core values in American education reflect those characteristics that support the political and economic systems that originally fueled education. Therefore, children in America receive rewards for following schedules, following directions, meeting deadlines, and obeying authority.

The most important value permeating the American classroom is **individualism**—the ideology that advocates the **liberty rights**, or independent action, of the individual. American students learn early, unlike their Japanese or Chinese counterparts, that society seeks out and reveres the best individual, whether that person achieves the best score on a test or the most points on the basketball court. Even collaborative activities focus on the leader, and team sports single out the one most valuable player of the year. The carefully constructed curriculum helps students develop their identities and **self-esteem**.

Conversely, Japanese students, in a culture that values community in place of individuality, learn to be ashamed if someone singles them out, and learn **social esteem**—how to bring honor to the group, rather than to themselves.

Going to school in a capitalist nation, American students also quickly learn the importance of **competition**, through both competitive learning games in the classroom, and through activities and athletics outside the classroom. Some kind of prize or reward usually motivates them to play, so students learn early to associate winning with possessing. Likewise, schools overtly teach patriotism, a preserver of political structure. Students must learn the Pledge of Allegiance and the stories of the nation's heroes and exploits. The need to instill patriotic values is so great that mythology often takes over, and teachers repeat stories of George Washington's honesty or Abraham Lincoln's virtue even though the stories themselves (such as Washington confessing to chopping down the cherry tree) may be untrue.

Another benefit that functionalists see in education is **sorting**— separating students on the basis of merit. Society's needs demand that the most capable people get channeled into the most important occupations. Schools identify the most capable students early. Those who score highest on classroom and standardized tests enter accelerated programs and college-preparation courses. Sociologists Talcott Parsons, Kingsley Davis, and Wilbert Moore referred to this as **social placement**. They saw this process as a beneficial function in society.

After sorting has taken place, the next function of education, **networking** (making interpersonal connections), is inevitable. People in high school and college network with those in similar classes and majors. This networking may become professional or remain personal. The most significant role of education in this regard is matchmaking. Sociologists primarily interest themselves in how sorting and networking lead couples together of similar backgrounds, interests, education, and income potential. People place so much importance on this function of education that some parents limit their children's options for college to insure that they attend schools where they can meet the "right" person to marry.

Functionalists point to the ironic dual role of education in both preserving and changing culture. Studies show that, as students progress through college and beyond, they usually become increasingly liberal as they encounter a variety of perspectives. Thus, more educated individuals are generally more liberal, while less educated people tend toward conservatism. Moreover, the heavy emphasis on research at most institutions of higher education puts them on the cutting edge of changes in knowledge, and, in many cases, changes in values as well. Therefore, while the primary role of education is to preserve and pass on knowledge and skills, education is also in the business of transforming them.

A final and controversial function assumed by education in the latter half of the twentieth century is **replacement of the family**. Many issues of career development, discipline, and human sexuality—once the domain of the family—now play a routine part in school curriculum. Parents who reject this function of education often choose to home-school their children or place them in private schools that support their values.

The conflict theory

Conflict theory sees the purpose of education as maintaining social inequality and preserving the power of those who dominate society. Conflict theorists examine the same functions of education as functionalists. Functionalists see education as a beneficial contribution to an ordered society; however, conflict theorists see the educational system as perpetuating the status quo by dulling the lower classes into being obedient workers.

Both functionalists and conflict theorists agree that the educational system practices sorting, but they disagree about how it enacts that sorting. Functionalists claim that schools sort based upon merit; conflict theorists argue that schools sort along distinct class and ethnic lines. According to conflict theorists, schools train those in the working classes to accept their position as a lower-class member of society. Conflict theorists call this role of education the "hidden curriculum."

Conflict theorists point to several key factors in defending their position. First, property taxes fund most schools; therefore, schools in affluent districts have more money. Such areas are predominantly white. They can afford to pay higher salaries, attract better teachers, and purchase newer texts and more technology. Students who attend these schools gain substantial advantages in getting into the best colleges and being tracked into higher-paying professions. Students in less affluent neighborhoods that do not enjoy these advantages are less likely to go to college and are more likely to be tracked into vocational or technical training. They also represent far higher numbers of minority students.

Conflict theorists contend that not only do the economics favor the white affluent, but so does school testing—particularly **IQ testing**, which schools can use to sort students. They argue that the tests, which claim to test intelligence, actually test cultural knowledge and therefore exhibit a cultural bias. For example, a question may ask: "Which one of these items belongs in an orchestra? A. accordion B. guitar C. violin D. banjo." This question assumes considerable cultural knowledge, including what an orchestra is, how it differs from a band, and what instruments comprise an orchestra. The question itself assumes exposure to a particular kind of music favored by white upper classes. Testing experts claim they have rid modern exams of such culturally biased questioning, but conflict theorists respond that cultural neutrality is impossible. All tests contain a knowledge base, and that knowledge base is always culturally sensitive.

Conflict theorists see education not as a social benefit or opportunity, but as a powerful means of maintaining power structures and creating a docile work force for capitalism.

The symbolic interactionist theory

Symbolic interactionists limit their analysis of education to what they directly observe happening in the classroom. They focus on how teacher expectations influence student performance, perceptions, and attitudes.

Robert Rosenthal and **Lenore Jacobson** conducted the landmark study for this approach in 1968. First, they examined a group of students with standard IQ tests. The researchers then identified a number of students who they said would likely show a sharp increase in abilities over the coming year. They informed the teachers of the results, and asked them to watch and see if this increase did occur. When the researchers repeated the IQ tests at the end of the year, the students identified by the researchers did indeed show higher IQ scores. The significance of this study lies in the fact that the researchers had randomly selected a number of average students. The researchers found that when the teachers expected a particular performance or growth, it occurred. This phenomenon, where a false assumption actually occurs because someone predicted it, is called a **self-fulfilling prophesy**. For example, the stock market may be stable with rising values. If investors become afraid that the market will crash, however, they may suddenly sell their stocks, which causes the market to crash. The crash occurred simply because investors feared it would do so.

Ray Rist conducted research similar to the Rosenthal-Jacobson study in 1970. In a kindergarten classroom where both students and teacher were African American, the teacher assigned students to tables based on ability; the "better" students sat at a table closer to her, the "average" students sat at the next table, and the "weakest" students sat at the farthest table. Rist discovered that the teacher assigned the students to a table based on the teacher's perception of the students' skill levels on the eighth day of class, without any form of testing to verify the placement. Rist also found that the students the teacher perceived as "better" learners came from higher social classes, while the "weak" students were from lower social classes.

Monitoring the students through the year, Rist found that the students closer to the teacher received the most attention and performed better. The farther from the teacher a student sat, the weaker that student performed. Rist continued the study through the next several years and found that the labels assigned to the students on the eighth day of kindergarten followed them throughout their schooling.

While symbolic-interactionist sociologists can document this process, they have yet to define the exact process of how teachers form their expectations or how students may communicate subtle messages to teachers about intelligence, skill, and so forth.

Reform of Education

In 1983, the National Commission on Excellence in Education issued a scathing review of American education titled "A Nation at Risk." Although the Commission did find some successes, the majority of the report focused on the failure of American education to prepare students for competing in a global market. Educational mediocrity, it claimed, caused lowered SAT (formerly the Scholastic Aptitude Test) scores, declining standards, grade inflation, poor performance in math and science, and functional illiteracy (reading and writing skills insufficient for daily living). The report also identified **social promotion**, which is the practice of promoting students who do not have basic skills to the next higher grade in order to preserve their self-esteem by continuing on with their classmates, as a culprit. Much of the discussion surrounding the report focused upon the lower SAT scores and **grade inflation**, which is the practice of assigning higher grades to lesser skills in order to support a normal grade curve. Educators defended education by arguing that the lower test scores resulted from more students with a wider grade range and narrower course loads taking the exams.

The report recommended sweeping reforms, first calling for higher standards with more course work in English, math, science, social studies, and computer science. Next, it demanded a stop to social promotion. Finally, the report pointed to below-average pay scales for teachers and recommended raising teacher salaries to attract more highly qualified teachers. In some cases, students entering teacher education programs were themselves the students with the lowest verbal and math scores.

Since the report, the United States has given increased funding and attention to education with mixed results. Many of the problems identified by the report continue. Social promotion continues because concern for the child's self-esteem often outweighs concern about the need for basic skills, and because an overburdened system cannot withstand holding back large numbers of students. Many states and districts have implemented programs to raise scores, and, although SAT scores have risen some, critics charge that revisions to the exam, which made it easier, caused the rise. Some districts have tied teachers' and administrators' salaries to student performance with mixed results. Myriad other issues that confront educators before educators reach the classroom, such as lack of teaching resources and even fear of student violence, further complicate education reform.

The Global Perspective on Education

Increasing global commerce and competition provides much of the fuel that drives the call for education reform. Many more nations are industrializing and competing in the global market. The nations with the best minds and best education will lead the world economically. When researchers compare the performance of American students to their international counterparts, the United States scores low compared to other industrialized nations. In a frequently quoted study, 13-year-olds in Korea and Taiwan scored highest in math and science exams. Thirteen-year-olds in the United States scored near the bottom of industrialized nations.

Experts point to parental attitudes and school systems to explain the differences. Asian parents maintain far higher expectations of their children, push them harder, and more often credit their children's success to "hard work." American parents, on the other hand, generally harbor lower expectations, become satisfied with performance more quickly, and often credit their children's success to "talent."

School systems also differ. In France and England, public schools provide preschool to 3-year-old children. The Japanese school year can run 45 to 60 days longer than the average American school year, with much shorter breaks. Most Japanese students also attend *juku,* or "cram school," after school, where they study for several more hours with tutors to review and augment the day's schoolwork. Fierce competition exists because not all students can get into the universities, and getting into the best universities secures the student's and the family's future. Although Japanese students may out perform American ones, critics point to the high suicide rate and other social ills associated with the Japanese system.

Current Issues

A number of issues and controversies now face educators and communities. Among them are discipline and security; race, ethnicity, and equality; mainstreaming; and public versus private education.

Discipline and security

Expressions of violence have increased in the culture, and so has violence in the schools. In the past, only urban or poor inner-city schools worried about serious violence. With recent school shootings in small towns from Kentucky to Oregon, all U.S. schools and districts, however small, must now directly address the increased incidence of school violence. Teachers have found children as young as kindergarten coming to school armed.

Schools have reacted decisively. To reduce the threat from strangers or unauthorized persons, many have closed campuses. Others require all persons on campus to wear identification at all times. When the students themselves come to school armed, however, the schools have been forced to take more drastic measures. Many have installed metal detectors or conduct random searches. Although some people question whether the searches constitute illegal search and seizure, most parents, students, administrators, and teachers feel that, given the risk involved, the infringement on civil liberties is slight.

Educators recognize that metal detectors alone will not solve the problem. Society must address the underlying issues that make children carry weapons. Many schools include anger management and conflict resolution as part of the regular curriculum. They also make counseling more available, and hold open forums to air differences and resolve conflicts.

School uniforms constitute another strategy for reducing violence, and public schools across the country—large and small—are beginning to require them. Many violent outbursts relate to gangs. Gang members usually wear identifying clothing, such as a particular color, style, or garment. By requiring uniforms and banning gang colors and markers, administrators can prevent much of the violence in the schools. Advocates point out, too, that uniforms reduce social class distinctions and cost less than buying designer wardrobes or standard school clothes.

Race, ethnicity, and equality
The first major examination of race, ethnicity, and equality in education came as part of the civil rights movement. Ordered by Congress, the Commissioner of Education appointed sociologist **James Coleman** to assess educational opportunities for people with diverse backgrounds. His team amassed information from 4,000 schools, 60,000 teachers, and about 570,000 students. The subsequent **Coleman Report** produced unexpected—and controversial—results, unforeseen even by researchers. The report concluded that the key

predictors of student performance were social class, family background and education, and family attitudes toward education. The Coleman Report pointed out that children coming from poor, predominantly non-white communities began school with serious deficits and many could not overcome them. According to the report, school facilities, funding, and curriculum played only minimal roles.

Some studies supported the Coleman Report's findings, while others disputed them. Studies by Rist and Rosenthal-Jacobson (discussed earlier in this chapter in the section on the symbolic-interactionist theory) demonstrated that specific classroom practices, such as teacher attention, did affect student performance. Sociologists reconcile the opposite findings by pointing out that Coleman's large-scale study reveals broad cultural patterns, while classroom studies are more sensitive to specific interactions. Sociologists conclude, then, that all of the factors named by the divergent studies do play a role in student success. No matter how different the study results, all researchers agree that a measurable difference exists between the performance of affluent white students and their poorer, non-white counterparts.

Even though researchers widely disputed the Coleman Report, the report did bring about two major changes:

- First was the development of **Head Start**, a federal program for providing academically focused preschool to low-income children. This program is specifically designed to compensate for the disadvantages that low-income students face. Head Start has proven successful, and most students who go through the program as 4- or 5-year-olds continue to perform better than students not enrolled in Head Start, at least through the sixth grade.

- The other consequence of the Coleman Report proved to be less successful and far more controversial than the Head Start program. In an effort to desegregate education, courts ordered some districts to institute **busing**—a program of transporting students to schools outside their neighborhoods, that they normally would not attend, in order to achieve racial balance.

This generally meant busing white students to inner-city schools and busing minority students to suburban schools. Public opposition to busing programs remains high, and the program has achieved only modest results.

Bilingual education, which means offering instruction in a language other than English, constitutes another attempt to equalize education for minority students. Federally mandated in 1968, bilingual education has generated considerable debate. Supporters argue that students whose first language is not English deserve an equal educational opportunity unavailable to them unless they can receive instruction in their first language. Opponents counter that students not taught in English will lack the fluency needed to function in daily life. Numerous studies support conclusions on both sides of the issue, and, as funding becomes scarce, the debate will intensify.

Mainstreaming

Mainstreaming is the practice of placing physically, emotionally, or mentally challenged students in a regular classroom instead of a special education classroom. Educators continue to debate the merits and problems of mainstreaming. In general, the practice seems to work best for students who can still keep pace with their peers in the classroom, and less well for students with more severe challenges. Experts note that exceptions do occur on both accounts and recommend careful consideration on a case-by-case basis.

Public versus private

Most of the public-versus-private discussion centers on public education. One cannot ignore the effect of private education and home schooling on American education, however. Many parents who are dissatisfied with the quality of public education, who are afraid of rising violence in the schools, or who want specific personal or religious values integrated into the curriculum, turn to private and parochial schools. The majority of private schools are religious, with the majority of those being Catholic.

Studies have found that private schools maintain higher expectations and that students in these schools generally outperform their public school peers. These findings support the Rist and Rosenthal-Jacobson studies.

Because of the success of private schools in educating at-risk students, more parents are seeking ways to afford these institutions, which have been largely available only to affluent white families who can pay the tuition costs. One proposed solution is a **voucher system**. The government would issue parents credit worth a dollar amount to take to the school of their choice, public or private. Advocates argue that this program would make private schooling more available to poorer families and create more equal opportunities. Critics charge that such a policy would drain public schools of needed funding and further erode public schools. The vouchers would not cover the entire cost of private school, and therefore still would not put private schooling within the reach of poorer families. The program would result, opponents argue, in further segregation of schooling. Other public school solutions include *magnet schools* that provide a selective academically demanding education and superior facilities for qualified students, *charter schools* that offer flexible and innovative education independent of the traditional rules and regulations governing public schools, and *interdistrict* and *intradistrict enrollments* that permit any eligible student in one school district to apply for enrollment in any district school or program.

Adulthood is primarily a time of determining lifestyles and developing relationships. Among other things, most adults eventually leave their parents' home, develop a long-term romantic relationship, and start a family, creating a new home.

Research by sociologist **Daniel Levinson** determined the stages of adult development, as presented in Table 12-1.

Table 12-1: Levinson's Stages of Adult Development

Age	Levinson's Stage
17-33	Novice phase of early adulthood
17-22	Early adult transition
22-28	Entering the adult world
28-33	Age-30 transition
33-45	Culmination of early adulthood
33-40	Settling down
40-45	Midlife transition
45-50	Entering middle adulthood
50-55	Age-50 transition
55-60	Culmination of middle adulthood
60-65	Late adult transition
65+	Late adulthood

These stages are generally accepted by researchers today in seeking to explain and evaluate adult development.

Early Adulthood (17-45)

An important aspect of achieving intimacy with another person is first being able to separate from the **family of origin**, or family of procreation. Most young adults have some familial attachments, but are also in the process of separating from them. This process normally begins during Daniel Levinson's **early adult transition** (17-22), when many young adults first leave home to attend college or take a job in another city.

By age 22 young adults have attained at least some level of attitudinal, emotional, and physical independence. They are ready for Levinson's **entering the adult world** (22-28) stage of early adulthood, during which relationships take center stage.

Relationships in Early Adulthood

Love, intimacy, and adult relationships go hand-in-hand. Psychologist **Robert Sternberg** proposed that **love** consists of three components: *passion, decision/commitment,* and *intimacy.* **Passion** concerns the intense feelings of physiological arousal and excitement (including sexual arousal) present in a relationship, while **decision/commitment** concerns the decision to love the partner and maintain the relationship. **Intimacy** concerns the sense of warmth and closeness in a loving relationship, including the desires to help the partner, to self-disclose, and to keep the partner in one's life. People express intimacy in three ways:

- **Physical intimacy** involves mutual affection and sexual activity.

- **Psychological intimacy** involves sharing feelings and thoughts.

- **Social intimacy** involves enjoying the same friends and types of recreation.

The many varieties of love described by Sternberg consist of varying degrees of passion, commitment, and intimacy. For example, **infatuation**, or "puppy love"—so characteristic of adolescence—involves passion, but not intimacy or commitment.

In addition to love and intimacy, sexuality is realized during young adulthood within the context of one or more relationships, whether long- or short-term. Although adolescent sexuality is of a growing and maturing nature, adult sexuality is fully expressive. The following sections discuss some of the more familiar types of adult relationships.

Singlehood

Today, many people are choosing **singlehood**, or the "single lifestyle." Regardless of their reasons for not marrying, many singles clearly lead satisfying and rewarding lives. Many claim that singlehood gives them personal control over their living space and freedom from interpersonal obligations. Today the number of singles in the United States remains at about 26 percent of men and 19 percent of women in the 1990s staying single for at least a portion of adulthood. Eventually, approximately 95 percent of Americans will marry.

Most singles date; many are sexually active, with the preferred sexual activities for singles remaining the same as those for other adults. Some singles choose **celibacy**—abstaining from sexual relationships.

Cohabitation and marriage

Cohabitation and **marriage** comprise the two most common long-term relationships of adulthood. Cohabitors are unmarried people who live together and have sex together. More than 3 million Americans (most between the ages of 25 and 45) cohabitate. Many individuals claim that they cohabitate as a test for marital compatibility, even though no solid evidence supports the idea that cohabitation increases later marital satisfaction. In contrast, some research suggests a relationship between premarital cohabitation and increased divorce rates. Other individuals claim that they cohabitate as an alternative to marriage, not as a trial marriage.

The long-term relationship most preferred by Americans is marriage. More than 90 percent of Americans will marry at least once, the average age for first-time marriage being 24 for females and 26 for males.

Marriage can be advantageous. Married people tend toward healthier and happier lives than their never-married, divorced, and widowed counterparts. On average, married males live longer than single males. Marriages seem happiest in the early years, although marital satisfaction increases again in the later years after parental responsibilities end and finances stabilize.

Marriage can also be disadvantageous. Numerous problems and conflicts arise in long-term relationships. Unrealistic expectations about marriage, as well as differences over sex, finances, household responsibilities, and parenting, create only a few of the potential problem areas.

As dual-career marriages become more common, so do potential complications. If one spouse refuses to assist, the other spouse may become stressed over managing a career, taking care of household chores, and raising the children. As much as Americans may hate to admit this fact, women in our culture still bear the primary responsibilities of child rearing. Conflicting demands may partly explain why married women with children leave their jobs more often than childless and single women.

Multiple roles, however, can be positive and rewarding. If of sufficient quality, these roles may lead to increased self-esteem, feelings of independence, and a greater sense of fulfillment.

Extramarital relationships

Severe problems in a marriage may lead one or both spouses to engage in **extramarital affairs**. *Nonconsensual* extramarital sexual activity (not agreed upon in advance by both married partners) constitutes a violation of commitment and trust between spouses. Whatever the reasons, nonconsensual affairs can irreparably damage a marriage. Marriages in which one or both partners "cheat" typically end in divorce. Some couples may choose to stay together for monetary reasons or until the children move out. On the other hand, *consensual* extramarital sexual activity ("swinging") involves both partners consenting to relationships outside of the marriage. Some couples find this to be an acceptable solution to their marital difficulties, while others find it to be detrimental to the long-term viability of their marriage.

Divorce

When significant problems in a relationship arise, some couples decide on **divorce**, or the legal termination of a marriage. About 50 percent of all marriages in the United States end in divorce, the average duration of these marriages is about 7 years.

Both the process and aftermath of divorce place great stress on both partners. Divorce can lead to increased risk of experiencing financial hardship, developing medical conditions (for example, ulcers) and mental problems (anxiety, depression), having a serious accident, attempting suicide, or dying prematurely. The couple's children and the extended families also suffer during a divorce, especially when disagreements over custody of the children ensue. Most divorcees, their children, and their families eventually cope. About 75 percent of divorcees remarry, and most of these second marriages remain intact until the death of one of the spouses.

Friends

Friends play an important role in the lives of young adults. Most human relationships, including casual acquaintances, are *nonloving* in that they do not involve true passion, commitment, or intimacy. According to Sternberg, intimacy, but not passion or commitment, characterizes **friendships**. In other words, closeness and warmth exist without feelings of passionate arousal and permanence. Friends normally come from similar backgrounds, share the same interests, and enjoy each other's company.

Although many young adults feel the time pressures of going to school, working, and starting a family, they usually manage to maintain at least some friendships, though perhaps with difficulty. As life responsibilities increase, time for socializing with others may be at a premium.

Adult friendships tend to be same-sex, non-romantic relationships. Adults often characterize their friendships as involving respect, trust, understanding, and acceptance—typically the same features as romantic relationships, but without the passion and intense commitment. Friendships also differ according to gender. Females tend to be more relational in their interactions, confiding their problems and feelings to other females. Males, on the other hand, tend to minimize confiding about their problems and feelings; instead, they seek out common-interest activities with other males.

Friends provide a healthy alternative to family members and acquaintances. They can offer emotional and social support, a different perspective, and a change of pace from daily routines.

Deciding to Start a Family in Early Adulthood

As young adults enter the **culminating phase of early adulthood (33-45)**, they enter the **settling down** (33-40) stage. By this time, they have established a career (at least the first one!) and found a spouse. If the couple have not already done so, they will probably decide to have one or more children and start a family.

People generally think that parenthood strengthens marriages, even though research indicates that marital satisfaction often declines after the birth of the first child. This need not be the case, however. If the marriage is already positive and the spouses share equally in parenting duties, they can minimize the hassles of parenthood and keep it from significantly interfering with marital happiness.

Regardless of the many joys of parenthood, new parents are not always prepared for the responsibility and time-commitment that raising a child requires, especially when the pregnancy is accidental rather than planned, or when the child is "difficult" and prone to irritability and excessive crying.

The postponement of marriage and childbearing until the 30s makes for an interesting trend in today's world. Two advantages of waiting are the emotional maturity of both partners and the stability of their relationship. A more mature and stable couple possesses the necessary tools for weathering the storms of parenthood. Another advantage is financial stability due to more years on the job, promotions, and long-term savings.

Another interesting trend is an increase in **nontraditional family units**. Examples of these include **blended families** (or "stepfamilies," in which children from previous marriages are "blended" into a new family), **single-parent families**, and **same-sex families**.

Some couples choose to remain childless. Couples who have children do not necessarily regard themselves as more "fulfilled" than couples who do not. The critical factor seems to be the couples' ability to choose their lifestyle.

Sources of information about family planning, conception, birth control, and other pregnancy options include the Planned Parenthood Federation of America, the National Right to Life Committee, and National Abortions Rights Action League.

Relationships in Middle Adulthood (45-65)

By middle age, more than 90 percent of adults have married at least once. Married people often describe their marital satisfaction in terms of a "U-curve." People generally affirm that their marriages are happiest during the early years, but not as happy during the middle years. Marital satisfaction then increases in the later years after finances have stabilized and parenting responsibilities have ended. Couples who stay together until after the last child leaves home will probably remain married for at least another 20 years as long as their intent was not to wait until the last child leaves the home to divorce.

Divorce

Middle adults do not exhibit an immunity to problems in relationships. Again, about 50 percent of all marriages in the United States end in divorce, with the median duration of these marriages being about 7 years. And of those that do last, marital bliss is not always a prominent feature. Why do so many marriages dissolve, and can spouses do anything to ensure that things work out?

Relationships dissolve for as many reasons as there are numbers of relationships. In some cases, the couple cannot handle an extended crisis. In other cases, the spouses change and grow in different directions. In still others, the spouses are completely incompatible from the very start. Long-term relationships rarely end because of difficulties with just one of the partners. Conflicts, problems, growing out of love, and "empty nest" (feeling a lack of purpose in life or emotional stress in response to all the children leaving home) issues inevitably involve both parties.

The course of love changes over time, and these changes may become evident by middle adulthood. The ideal form of love in adulthood involves the three components of passion, intimacy, and commitment—called **consummate love**, or complete love. This type of love is unselfish, devoted, and most often associated with romantic relationships. Unfortunately, achieving consummate love, as Sternberg noted, is similar to losing weight. Getting started is easy; sticking to it is much harder.

For many middle-age couples, passion fades as intimacy and commitment build. In other words, many middle adults find themselves in a marriage typified by **companionate love**, which is both committed and intimate but not passionate. Yet love need not be this way, nor do such changes necessitate the end of a long-term relationship. In contrast, many middle adult couples find effective ways of improving their ability to communicate, increasing emotional intimacy, rekindling the fires of passion, and growing together. The understanding that evolves between two people over time can be wonderful.

For others, the end of passion signals the end of the relationship. Passion enamors some people to such a degree that they do not approach their loving relationships realistically. This observation especially holds true for those who base their relationships on infatuation or the assumption that "true love" takes care of all conflicts and problems. When the flames of passion die out (which is inevitable in many cases) or the going gets rough, these spouses decide to move on to a new relationship. Divorce and extramarital relationships are but two consequences of marital unhappiness and dissatisfaction.

Interpersonal disagreements may increase as the couple becomes better acquainted and intimate. People who never learned how to communicate their concerns and needs effectively with their spouse or how to work through conflicts are more likely to become separated or divorced. Most couples quarrel and argue, but few know how to work at resolving conflicts equitably.

Relationships that last

What characteristics predict if a loving relationship will thrive or die? Long-term relationships share several factors, including both partners regarding the relationship as a long-term commitment; both verbally and physically expressing appreciation, admiration, and love; both offering emotional support; and both considering each other as a best friend.

Essential to preserving a quality relationship is the couple's deciding to practice **effective communication**. Communication establishes and nurtures intimacy within a relationship, helping partners to better relate to and understand each other. Intimacy helps them feel close, connected, and loved, and creates an atmosphere of mutual cooperation for active decision-making and problem solving. Communicating realistically leads to a satisfying and healthy relationship, regardless of the relationship's level of development.

Friends

In all age groups, friends provide a healthy alternative to family and acquaintances. They offer support, direction, guidance, and a change of pace from usual routines. Although many young adults manage to maintain at least some friendships, family, school, and work can become greater concerns for middle adults. Life responsibilities reach an all-time high, so time for socializing is often at an exceptional premium. For this reason, middle adults generally maintain fewer close friendships than their newlywed and retired counterparts, although this is not always the case. Yet where quantity is lacking, quality predominates. People often nourish some of the closest ties between friends during middle adulthood.

Children

As adults wait later to marry and start families, more and more middle adults find themselves raising small children. This is not the typical pattern, however. By the time most parents reach middle age, their children are at least of adolescent age.

Ironically, middle adults and their adolescent children often both experience emotional crises. For adolescents the crisis involves the search for their own identities as separate from their family members; for middle adults, the search is for **generativity**, or fulfillment through such activities as raising children, working, or creating. These two crises are not always compatible, as parents try to deal with their own issues as well as those of their adolescents (for example, discovering identity).

Some middle adults begin to "live out" their own youthful fantasies through their children. They may try to make their teenage children into improved versions of themselves.

Witnessing their children on the verge of becoming adults can trigger a **midlife crisis**. The adolescent journey into young adulthood reminds middle-age parents of their own aging processes and the inescapable settling into middle and later adulthood. As a result, parents may experience depression or seek to recapture their youth through age-inappropriate behavior and sexual adventures.

Some teenagers ignite so much tension at home that their departure to college or into a career acts as a relief to parents. Other parents experience the **empty nest syndrome** after all of their children leave home. Without the children as a focal point for their lives, they have trouble reconnecting to each other and rediscovering their own individuality separate from parenthood.

In recent decades, Americans have witnessed the phenomenon of grown children staying or returning home to live with their parents. Whether they choose to stay at home for financial or emotional reasons, adult children who live with their parents can cause difficulty for all parties. Parents may delay their own "getting reacquainted" stage while managing a "not-so-empty nest," and their adult children may have to adjust to social isolation and problems establishing intimacy with significant others of their own age. Adult children living at home may also shirk necessary adult responsibilities. This "adult-child-living-with-the-parents" arrangement tends to work best when both parties agree upon it as a temporary situation, and when the child is less than 25.

Middle-age parents typically maintain close relationships with their grown children who have left home. However, many parents report feeling as if they continue to give more than they receive from their relationships with their children. This can be all the more the case for "sandwich" generation middle-agers who must also tend to the needs of their own aging parents.

Parents

Most middle adults characterize the relationship with their parents as affectionate. Indeed a strong bond often exists between related middle and older adults. Although the majority of middle adults do not live with their parents, they usually maintain frequent and positive contact. And, perhaps for the first time, middle adults see their parents as fallible human beings.

One issue facing middle adults is that of caring for their aging parents. In some cases, adults, who expected to spend their middle-age years traveling and enjoying their own children and grandchildren, instead find themselves taking care of their ailing parents. Relationships with older adult parents vary a great deal. Some parents remain completely independent of their adult children's support; others partially depend upon their children; and still others completely depend upon them. Daughters and daughters-in-law most commonly take care of aging parents and in-laws.

Support groups and counseling exist for adults caring for their older parents. These typically provide information, teach caregiver skills, and offer emotional support. Other programs, such as Social Security and Medicare, ease the financial burdens of older adults and their caregivers.

Middle adults normally react with intensity and pain to the death of one or both parents. (Of course, this holds true for individuals at all stages of the lifespan.) The death of one's parents ends a life-long relationship and offers a "wake-up call" to live life to its fullest and mend broken relationships while the people involved still live. Finally, the death serves as a reminder of one's own mortality.

Even though the death of a parent is never welcome, some long-term adult caretakers express certain ambivalent feelings about the event.

Relationships in Older Adulthood (65 and Older)

Given increases in longevity, today's older adults face the possibility of acquiring and maintaining relationships far longer than during any other time in modern history. For instance, nearly 1 in 10 adults over the age of 65 has a child who is at least age 65. Nurturing long-term family relationships can bring both rewards and challenges. Over the decades, sibling rivalry may disappear and give way to peaceful relationships, while younger adults may feel the strain of trying to care for their aging and ailing parents, grandparents, and other relatives. Still, most young people report satisfying relationships with their older family members.

Marriage and family
People sometimes refer to older adult marriages and families as "retirement marriages" or "retirement families." In such families the following demographics typically hold true:

- The average age of the wife is 68, and the husband, 71.

- Their previous marriages had lasted for more than 40 years, and they had high levels of marital satisfaction.

- They have three grown children, the oldest being about 40.

- Even though they consider themselves retired, 20 percent of the husbands and 4 percent of the wives continue to work.

The typical household income is less than in earlier stages of the lifespan, often translating into a decrease in standard of living.

Widowhood, or the disruption of marriage due to death of the spouse, presents by far the most devastating event in older adult marriages. Nearly 3 percent of men ("widowers") and 12 percent of women ("widows") in the United States are widowed. In the 75 and older age group, approximately 25 percent of men and 66 percent of women are widowed.

Widows and widowers commonly complain of the difficulty that they experience finding a new spouse or partner. This especially holds true for widows, who must contend with the social stigmas of being "old" and "asexual." Widows tend to outnumber widowers in retirement communities, assisted living facilities, and nursing homes.

Relationships with adult children

The majority of older Americans—80 to 90 percent—have grown children, and enjoy frequent contact with them. Contrary to popular misconception, although the elderly enjoy these contacts they do not want to live with their grown children. Instead, they want to live in their own homes and remain independent for as long as possible. Typically, they would rather move into a private room in an assisted-living facility or group home than move in with their children. At any one time, only about 5 percent of adults over age 65 live in an institution. More than 75 percent of institutionalized older adults, however, live within an hour's drive of one of their children.

As for the quality of the relationship between older adults and their grown children, most research suggests that the elderly rate their experiences as positive. This particularly holds true when they have good health, enjoy common interests (such as church, holidays, hobbies), and share similar views (on politics, religion, child rearing, and so forth) with their children. The elderly do not necessarily rate as positive frequent contacts with their children when these contacts come from long-term illness or family problems (a daughter's divorce, for example).

The potential for **elderly abuse**, or the neglect and/or physical and emotional abuse of dependent elderly persons, creates one very disturbing aspect of older adulthood. Neglect may take the form of withholding food or medications, not changing bed linens, or failing to provide proper hygienic conditions. Physical abuse may occur as striking, shoving, shaking, punching, or kicking the elderly. Emotional abuse may take the form of verbal threats, swearing, and insults. Estimates are that approximately 5 percent of American older adults receive abuse each year.

Elderly abuse can occur in institutions, but more commonly takes place in the homes of the older person's spouse, children, and grandchildren. The typical victim is an older adult who is in poor health and lives with someone else. In fact, the person who lives alone has a low risk of becoming a victim of this form of abuse.

Both victims and abusers require treatment, whether individual, family, or group therapy. The main goal, however, is ensuring the safety of the elderly victim. The law requires many licensed professionals, such as clinical psychologists, to report known cases of elderly abuse to the authorities.

Grandparenting

On average, men become grandfathers at age 52, and women become grandmothers at age 50. Therefore, grandparenting hardly restricts itself to older adults.

Although idealizing grandparenting is easy to do, the quality of grandparent-grandchild relationships varies across and within families. Generally, the majority of grandparents report having warm and loving relationships with their grandchildren. In addition to helping their grandchildren develop an appreciation for the past, positive grandparenting helps older adults avoid isolation and dependence while finding additional meaning and purpose in life. Grandparenting also facilitates personality development in later life by allowing older adults opportunities to reexamine and rework the tasks of earlier psychosocial stages.

Friendships

Having close friends in later life, as in any other period of life, consistently corresponds with happiness and satisfaction. Friends provide support, companionship, and acceptance, which are crucial to most older adults' sense of self-esteem. They provide opportunities to trust, confide, and share mutually enjoyed activities. They also seem to protect against stress, physical and mental problems, and premature death.

Because older men more likely rely on their wives for companionship, older women typically enjoy a wider circle of close friends. Older men, however, develop more other-gender friendships, probably because women generally live longer that men, meaning more women than men are available for such friendships. When older women can find available men with whom to be friends, they may hesitate to become too close. This is especially true if either are married. These women may also worry about what others are thinking, as they do not want to appear improper or forward.

Homosexual and Bisexual Relationships

Some couples do not fit into traditional models of marriage and family. A person who is attracted to members of the opposite sex is **heterosexual**, or "straight." A person who is attracted to members of the same sex is **homosexual**, or "gay" (male) or "lesbian" (female). And a person who is attracted to members of both sexes is **bisexual**, or "bi."

Although the United States does not legally recognize same-sex marriages or unions, homosexuals and bisexuals (like heterosexuals) enjoy a variety of relationships. They live together, alone, with family or friends, or have housemates. They also come from all walks of life, socioeconomic levels, and backgrounds. Making generalizations about homosexual or bisexual relationships—romantic, social, working, or otherwise—is difficult, as is making generalizations about heterosexual relationships.

Relationship categories

Nonetheless, in the 1970s, researchers **A. P. Bell** and **M. S. Weinberg** studied nearly 1,000 gays and lesbians and found that about 75 percent fell into one of the following relationship categories:

- **Asexual homosexuals** are single, have few or no sex partners, and would probably be considered sexually withdrawn.

- **Dysfunctional homosexuals** are single, have many sex partners, but also have sexual problems and/or regrets about being homosexual.

- **Functional homosexuals** are single, have many sex partners, and have few or no sexual problems or regrets about being homosexual.

- **Open-coupled relationships** involve one-on-one relationships, but both partners have a number of sex partners.

- **Close-coupled relationships** resemble monogamous heterosexual marriages.

As the above categories show, homosexual relationships are diverse.

Sociologists estimate that between 40 and 60 percent of homosexuals maintain committed relationships. Gay and lesbian couples may stay together for as many years as heterosexual couples. Also like heterosexuals, they may or may not find satisfaction in such relationships.

Children

Many homosexual couples decide to raise children. Researchers suggest that children brought up in homosexual homes do not differ from children brought up in heterosexual homes in terms of intelligence, gender role, gender identity, or general life adjustment. Researchers also suggest that children from homosexual homes are no more likely to become homosexuals themselves than are children from heterosexual homes.

The variety and number of religious organizations and beliefs around the world is so large that sociologists have a difficult time arriving at a single definition of religion. In Western societies, people usually identify religion with Christianity: the belief in Jesus Christ as the Son of God who promises salvation through faith and life after death. Yet religion as a global phenomenon presents a much more complex picture, because most of the world's religions lack the core concepts of Christianity.

To avoid thinking about religion from a culturally biased point of view, sociologists first define what religion is *not*.

- First, religion is not necessarily **monotheistic**, which is the belief in monotheism, or a single deity. Instead, many religions embrace **polytheism**, or the belief in multiple deities. Still other religions, such as Confucianism, recognize no gods at all.

- Religion is not necessarily a body of moral rules and demands concerning the behavior of believers. The notion that deities somehow keep track of how believers behave is foreign to many religions.

- Religion is not necessarily a belief in the supernatural, heaven, hell, or even life after death. Confucianism, again as an example, emphasizes acceptance of the natural harmony of the world, not finding truths that lie beyond it.

- Finally, religion is not necessarily an explanation of the origins of creation. The Christian story of Adam and Eve explains the origins of humanity. Many religions, but not all, have similar myths of origin.

Having examined what religion is not, sociologists consider what characteristics do constitute religion. Sociologists generally define **religion** as a codified set of moral beliefs concerning sacred things and rules governing the behavior of believers who form a spiritual community. All religions share at least some characteristics. Religions use symbols, invoke feelings of awe and reverence, and prescribe rituals for their adherents to practice. Religion differs from **magic**, which involves superstitious beliefs and behaviors designed to bring about a desired end.

Religion has numerous rituals and ceremonies, which may include lighting candles, holding processions, kneeling, praying, singing hymns and psalms, chanting, listening to sacred readings, eating certain foods, fasting from other foods on special days, and so forth. These rituals, because of their religious nature, may differ quite a bit from the procedures of ordinary daily life. Religious individuals may practice their rituals and ceremonies alone, at home, or within special spaces: shrines, temples, churches, synagogues, or ceremonial grounds.

In most traditional societies, religion plays a central role in cultural life. People often synthesize religious symbols and rituals into the material and artistic culture of the society: literature, storytelling, painting, music, and dance. The individual culture also determines the understanding of *priesthood*. A **priest** offers sacrifices to a deity or deities on behalf of the people. In smaller hunting-and-gathering societies no priesthood exists, although certain individuals specialize in religious (or magical) knowledge. One such specialist is the **shaman**, who the people believe controls supernatural forces. People may consult the shaman when traditional religion fails.

Totemism and Animism

Totemism and animism are religious forms common to smaller societies. A **totem** is any species of plants or animals thought to possess supernatural powers. Each group within the society may have its own totem, including associated ceremonies. Totemic beliefs may not be as foreign to the Western mind as first expected; many Westerners have totems. School mascots, symbols, and emblems all constitute totems.

Animism is the belief that spirits, apparitions, angels, or demons inhabit the earth. Either good or bad, these spirits interact with and/or influence humans in a variety of ways. For example, animists believe that malevolent spirits cause demonic possession, insanity, and disapproved behavior. From the animistic perspective, treating unsanctioned actions and attitudes requires praying to good forces and exorcising evil ones. Animism is not limited to small, simple, pre-industrial societies; various Americans in the 1990s believe in the existence of supernatural entities that influence humans.

Judaism, Christianity, and Islam

As societies become larger and more complex, its people become more likely to join monotheistic religions. The three most influential monotheistic religions in world history are *Judaism, Christianity,* and *Islam,* all of which began in the Middle East.

Judaism
Judaism dates from about 1200 B.C. The first Hebrews were nomads who settled in the land of Canaan near Egypt. Unlike their polytheistic neighbors, the Jewish *patriarchs* ("leaders") and *prophets* ("inspired" teachers) committed themselves to one almighty God.

They stressed utter obedience to Yahweh in the form of a strict moral code, or law.

Jews call their holy text the *Tenakh,* which Christians call the "Old Testament." Within the Tenakh lie the five books of the *Torah,* which begins with the creation of the world by God's word. The Torah primarily tells the story of the early Hebrews and Yaweh's communications to Moses, which established laws on worship and daily life.

The Torah plays a central role in Jewish worship. During services in the synagogue, the rabbi removes the Torah (rolled into a scroll) from the ark (a cupboard). The rabbi then carries the scroll, capped with a silver crown, in procession to a lectern, opens it, and reads from it to the congregation.

Christianity
Christians believe that Jesus Christ is the Son of God and the "Messiah" (meaning "Christ" and "Annointed One") who saves the world. This global religion first emerged as a sect of Judaism, and in the beginning embraced many Judaic views and practices. Within decades of Jesus' death, Christians began distinguishing themselves from their Jewish neighbors. Much of Christianity's rapid growth in the early years was due to a Greek-speaking Jew and Roman citizen named Saul of Tarsas. Later known as St. Paul, he preached extensively and planted churches in the Middle East, Turkey, and Greece. Because Christians refused to worship the Roman Emperor as divine, Romans severely persecuted Christians until the 4th century. At that time, Emperor Constantine made Christianity the official religion of the Roman State. Today, Christianity has grown into an influential force throughout the world, but especially in the West.

The Bible's (the 66 books of the Judeo-Christian Scriptures) "New Testament" (new covenant) is a collection of 26 books and letters interpreting portions of the Tenakh from a Christian point of view. The New Testament also presents a range of unique teachings, such as the writings of St. Paul, which early Christians sent to newly established churches. The authors of the Gospels, or presentations of Jesus' life and teachings, probably wrote them decades later, though contemporary Biblical scholarship on this topic remains inconclusive.

Christianity represents the largest of the world's religions and is also more evenly spread around the globe than any other religion. Christianity claims more than a billion adherents, though Christians belong to many different **denominations** (groups with a particular theology and form of organization) that sharply divide the religion. The three largest Christian denominations are Roman Catholicism, Eastern Orthodoxy, and Protestantism (which includes such denominations as Methodist, Presbyterian, Episcopalian, and Baptist).

Islam

The second largest religion in today's world is Islam, which originated from the teachings of the 7th century prophet Mohammed. His teachings most directly express the will of Allah, the one God of Islam. Moslems, or followers of the Islamic religion, believe that Allah also spoke through earlier prophets such as Jesus and Moses before enlightening Mohammed.

Moslems have five primary religious duties ("The Pillars of Islam"):

- Reciting the Islamic creed, which states that Allah is the one God and Mohammed is his son.

- Taking part in ceremonial washings and reciting formal prayers five times every day. During these prayers, worshippers always face towards the holy city of Mecca in Saudi Arabia.

- Observing of Ramadan—a month of fasting when Moslems may have no food or drink during daylight hours.

- Giving money to the poor.

- Making at least one pilgrimage to Mecca.

Messages that Mohammed received from Allah comprise the Islamic scriptures, called the Koran. ("Koran" derives from the Arabic term meaning "to recite.") Because the prophet could not write or read, he memorized Allah's words and later relayed them to his students. After Mohammed's death, his followers wrote down these revelations. The Koran sets forth standards of daily behavior and the Pillars of Islam.

Islam has grown to more than 600 million adherents throughout the world. Most Moslems live in the Middle East, Pakistan, and parts of Africa.

Hinduism, Buddhism, Confucianism, and Taoism

The four major religions of the Far East are *Hinduism, Buddhism, Confucianism,* and *Taoism.*

Hinduism

Hinduism, a polytheistic religion and perhaps the oldest of the great world religions, dates back about 6,000 years. Hinduism comprises so many different beliefs and rituals that some sociologists have suggested thinking of it as a grouping of interrelated religions.

Hinduism teaches the concept of **reincarnation**—the belief that all living organisms continue eternally in cycles of birth, death, and rebirth. Similarly, Hinduism teaches the **caste system**, in which a person's previous incarnations determine that person's hierarchical position in this life. Each caste comes with its own set of responsibilities and duties, and how well a person executes these tasks in the current life determines that person's position in the next incarnation.

Hindus acknowledge the existence of both male and female gods, but they believe that the ultimate divine energy exists beyond these descriptions and categories. The divine soul is present and active in all living things.

More than 600 million Hindus practice the religion worldwide, though most reside in India. Unlike Moslems and Christians, Hindus do not usually proselytize (attempt to convert others to their religion).

Buddhism, Confucianism, and Taoism

Three other religions of the Far East include *Buddhism, Confucianism, and Taoism.* These **ethical religions** have no gods like Yawheh or Allah, but espouse ethical and moral principles designed to improve the believer's relationship with the universe.

Buddhism originates in the teachings of the *Buddha,* or the "Enlightened One" (Siddhartha Gautama)—a 6th century B.C. Hindu prince of southern Nepal. Humans, according to the Buddha, can escape the cycles of reincarnation by renouncing their earthly desires and seeking a life of meditation and self-discipline. The ultimate objective of Buddhism is to attain **Nirvana**, which is a state of total spiritual satisfaction. Like Hinduism, Buddhism allows religious divergence. Unlike it, though, Buddhism rejects ritual and the caste system. While a global religion, Buddhism today most commonly lies in such areas of the Far East as China, Japan, Korea, Sri Lanka, Thailand, and Burma. A recognized "denomination" of Buddhism is *Zen Buddhism,* which attempts to transmit the ideas of Buddhism without requiring acceptance of all of the teachings of Buddha.

Confucius, or K'ung Futzu, lived at the same time as the Buddha. Confucius's followers, like those of Lao-tzu, the founder of Taoism, saw him as a moral teacher and wise man—not a religious god, prophet, or leader. Confucianism's main goal is the attainment of inner harmony with nature. This includes the veneration of ancestors. Early on, the ruling classes of China widely embraced Confucianism. Taoism shares similar principles with Confucianism. The teachings of Lao-tzu stress the importance of meditation and nonviolence as means of reaching higher levels of existence. While some Chinese still practice Confucianism and Taoism, these religions have lost much of their impetus due to resistance from today's Communist government. However, some concepts of Taoism, like reincarnation, have found an expression in modern "New Age" religions.

Sociological Theories of Religion

The ideas of three early sociological theorists continue to strongly influence the sociology of religion: Durkheim, Weber, and Marx.

Even though none of these three men was particularly religious, the power that religion holds over people and societies interested them all. They believed that religion is essentially an illusion; because culture and location influence religion to such a degree, the idea that religion presents a fundamental truth of existence seemed rather improbable to them. They also speculated that, in time, the appeal and influence of religion on the modern mind would lessen.

Durkheim and functionalism

Emile Durkheim, the founder of functionalism, spent much of his academic career studying religions, especially those of small societies. The totetism, or primitive kinship system of Australian aborigines as an "elementary" form of religion, primarily interested him. This research formed the basis of Durkheim's 1921 book, *The Elementary Forms of the Religious Life*, which is certainly the best-known study on the sociology of religion. Durkheim viewed religion within the context of the entire society and acknowledged its place in influencing the thinking and behavior of the members of society.

Durkheim found that people tend to separate religious symbols, objects, and rituals, which are sacred, from the daily symbols, objects, and routines of existence referred to as the profane. Sacred objects are often believed to have divine properties that separate them from profane objects. Even in more-advanced cultures, people still view sacred objects with a sense of reverence and awe, even if they do not believe that the objects have some special power.

Durkheim also argued that religion never concerns only belief, but also encompasses regular rituals and ceremonies on the part of a group of believers, who then develop and strengthen a sense of group solidarity. Rituals are necessary to bind together the members of a religious group, and they allow individuals to escape from the mundane aspects of daily life into higher realms of experience. Sacred rituals and ceremonies are especially important for marking occasions such as births, marriages, times of crisis, and deaths.

Durkheim's theory of religion exemplifies how functionalists examine sociological phenomena. According to Durkheim, people see religion as contributing to the health and continuation of society in general. Thus, religion functions to bind society's members by prompting them to affirm their common values and beliefs on a regular basis.

Durkheim predicted that religion's influence would decrease as society modernizes. He believed that scientific thinking would likely replace religious thinking, with people giving only minimal attention to rituals and ceremonies. He also considered the concept of "God" to be on the verge of extinction. Instead, he envisioned society as promoting **civil religion**, in which, for example, civic celebrations, parades, and patriotism take the place of church services. If traditional religion were to continue, however, he believed it would do so only as a means to preserve social cohesion and order.

Weber and social change
Durkheim claimed that his theory applied to religion in general, yet he based his conclusions on a limited set of examples. Max Weber, on the other hand, initiated a large-scale study of religions around the globe. His principal interest was in large, global religions with

millions of believers. He conducted in-depth studies of Ancient Judaism, Christianity, Hinduism, Buddhism, and Taoism. In *The Protestant Ethic and the Spirit of Capitalism* (1904/1958), Weber examined the impact of Christianity on Western thinking and culture.

The fundamental purpose of Weber's research was to discover religion's impact on social change. For example, in Protestantism, especially the "Protestant Work Ethic," Weber saw the roots of capitalism. In the Eastern religions, Weber saw barriers to capitalism. For example, Hinduism stresses attaining higher levels of spirituality by escaping from the toils of the mundane physical world. Such a perspective does not easily lend itself to making and spending money.

To Weber, Christianity was a *salvation religion* that claims people can be "saved" when they convert to certain beliefs and moral codes. In Christianity, the idea of "sin" and its atonement by God's grace plays a fundamental role. Unlike the Eastern religions' passive approach, salvation religions like Christianity are active, demanding continuous struggles against sin and the negative aspects of society.

Marx: Conflict theory

Despite his influence on the topic, Karl Marx was not religious and never made a detailed study of religion. Marx's views on the sociology of religion came from 19th century philosophical and theological authors such as Ludwig Feuerbach, who wrote *The Essence of Christianity* (1841). Feuerbach maintained that people do not understand society, so they project their own culturally based norms and values onto separate entities such as gods, spirits, angels, and demons. According to Feuerbach, after humans realize that they have projected their own values onto religion, they can achieve these values in this world rather than in an afterlife.

Marx once declared that religion is the "opium of the people." He viewed religion as teaching people to accept their current lot in life, no matter how bad, while postponing rewards and happiness to some afterlife. Religion, then, prohibits social change by teaching nonresistance to oppression, diverting people's attention away from worldly injustices, justifying inequalities of power and wealth for the privileged, and emphasizing rewards yet to come.

Although people commonly assume that Marx saw no place for religion, this assumption is not entirely true. Marx held that religion served as a sanctuary from the harshness of everyday life and oppression by the powerful. Still, he predicted that traditional religion would one day pass away.

Types of Religious Organizations

All religious organizations involve communities of believers. However, these communities come in different forms. The most basic of these today are *religious movements, denominations*, *sects,* and *cults*.

Religious movements and denominations

A form of social movement, **religious movements** involve groups of people who join together to spread a new religion or to reinterpret an old one. Religious movements are large and typically "open" in their memberships, especially at the beginning of the movement. Examples of religious movements include the early Christian movement, the Lutheran movement that began the Protestant Reformation, the Reformed Jewish movement, and, more recently, the Islamic Fundamentalist movement.

The agendas of many religious movements fade when their leaders lose influence, are replaced, or die. A movement that survives, though, may become a church, or *denomination*. In other words, the movement may become a formal organization of adherents with established symbols, rituals, and methods of governance.

Millennial movements periodically come on the scene, especially at the turn of centuries and millennia. Popular among some fringe Christian sects and cults, millennialists anticipate large-scale catastrophe, disaster, and social changes—perhaps in fulfillment of Scriptural prophecies. They may also look forward to the collective salvation for a particular group of believers—usually themselves.

Denominations are large and established religious bodies that have a hierarchy of religious leaders operating within a formal, bureaucratic structure. Most denominational members are born into and grow up within the body. Examples of Christian denominations include the Roman Catholic Church, the United Methodist Church, and the Antiochian Orthodox Church.

Sects and cults

Sects are smaller, less organized religious bodies of committed members. They typically arise in protest to a larger denomination, like the Anglicans originally did to the Roman church in the 1500s. They may have few or no leaders and little formal structure. Convinced that they have "the truth" and that no one else does (especially not the denomination against which they are protesting), sects actively seek new converts. People are more likely to join sects than to be born into them.

As sects grow, they may mellow and become an institutional religious body instead of a protesting group. If a sect survives over an extended period of time, it will probably become a denomination. In contrast to sects, denominations normally recognize each other as legitimate churches (though doctrinally in error) and peacefully coexist.

At first **cults** may resemble sects, but important differences exist. Cults, the most transient and informal of all religious groups, provide havens for people who reject the norms and values of larger society. Cultists may live separately or together in communes. Additionally, cults normally center around a charismatic leader who focuses on bringing together people of the same turn of mind. The potential for abuse and other problems in such environments has led American society to give much negative press to cults, although not all cults are necessarily abusive.

Social Correlates of Religion

Religious persuasion seems to relate to political persuasion. Jews and Catholics are more likely to be Democrats than are Protestants. Likewise, Jews tend to be more liberal than Catholics, who tend to be more liberal than Protestants. Membership of religious organizations also correlates positively with socioeconomic status. Baptists tend to be comparatively poor, whereas Anglicans, Presbyterians, and Jews tend to be wealthy. And Catholics, on average, have higher income than comparable members of Protestant denominations do. However, these generalizations are just that: general statements. You must interpret statistics with caution. For example, some of the poorest people in the United States belong to the Roman Catholic church, and considerable differences exist among members of the Protestant churches. Some of the wealthiest people now belong to the Church of Jesus Christ of Latter Day Saints (the "Mormons").

The vast majority of Americans—around 95 percent—say they have some form of religious beliefs: in God, heaven, the divine inspiration of Scriptures, and so on. Whereas 70 percent of Americans belong to religious organizations, only about 40 percent claim to attend weekly synagogue or church services. People in upper social groups, on average, attend church more regularly than those in other social groups. Similarly, Catholics, on average, attend church more regularly than Protestants. Members who actually attend services tend to actively participate within their congregations.

Religious Fundamentalism

One particularly notable feature of religion in the Unites Sates has been the appearance of fundamentalist religious groups. **Fundamentalism** refers to "black-and-white" thinking that opposes **modernism**, or progressive thinking about religion and other social topics. Fundamentalist groups tend to oppose anything that challenges their religious group's interpretations and opinions. For instance, Christian fundamentalists believe in the literal inerrancy of the Bible, and often define themselves as theologically and ritually conservative, or even "not Catholic." They see themselves as reacting against liberal theology.

To most Americans the term *fundamentalist* conjures up images of "Bible-thumping" Protestants, which is far from the case. All denominations and groups—including those of religions like Islam—contain fundamentalist members. These activists usually think that they have a corner on "the truth," and do not tolerate other viewpoints or practices.

The most well-known fundamentalist denominations in the United States are the Assemblies of God, the Southern Baptist Convention, and the Seventh-Day Adventists. Organizations such as these often become politically active, and support the conservative political "right," including groups like the Moral Majority.

Health is a state of complete well-being: physical, mental, and emotional. This definition emphasizes the importance of being more than disease free, and recognizes that a healthy body depends upon a healthy environment and a stable mind. **Medicine** is the social institution that diagnoses, treats, and prevents disease. To accomplish these tasks, medicine depends upon most other sciences—including life and earth sciences, chemistry, physics, and engineering. **Preventive medicine** is a more recent approach to medicine, which emphasizes health habits that prevent disease, including eating a healthier diet, getting adequate exercise, and insuring a safe environment.

Sociological Perspective on Health

Sociology assumes that a functioning society depends upon healthy people and upon controlling illness. In examining social constructs of health and illness, sociologist Talcott Parsons identified what he called "**the sick role**," or the social definition of, the behavior of, and the behavior toward those whom society defines as ill. Parsons identified four components to the sick role.

The sick person is

- Not held responsible for being sick.
- Not responsible for normal duties.
- Not supposed to like the role.
- Supposed to seek help to get out of the role.

Society allows those who fulfill these criteria to assume the sick role, but society loses sympathy for and denies the role to those who appear to like it or those who do not seek treatment. In other cases, family and friends may show sympathy for a while, but lose patience with the victim and assume he or she is seeking attention or is a hypochondriac.

Although many believe that science alone determines illness, this sociological view points out that society determines sickness as well. For example, the culture defines diseases as legitimate if they have a clear "scientific" or laboratory diagnosis, such as cancer or heart disease. In the past, society considered conditions such as chemical dependency, whether drug- or alcohol-based, as character weaknesses, and denied those who suffered from addiction the sick role. Today, drug rehabilitation programs and the broader culture generally recognize addictions as a disease, even though the term "disease" is medically contested. In today's culture, addicts may take on the sick role as long as they seek help and make progress toward getting out of the sick role.

In the past, society first dismissed or judged various ailments, only to later recognize the ailments as legitimate. People now recognize premenstrual syndrome (PMS)—once considered female hypochondria—as a legitimate, treatable hormonal condition. Acquired Immunodeficiency Syndrome, or AIDS, first emerged in the early 1980s in the male homosexual community. Because of the disease's early association with a lifestyle many people considered immoral, society granted those who acquired the disease little to no sympathy and denied them the sick role. People punished these victims for violating the norms and values of the society, rather than recognizing them as legitimately ill. As society became more knowledgeable about the disease, and as the disease affected a broader portion of the population, attitudes toward AIDS and those afflicted changed as well.

Today some conditions still struggle for recognition as legitimate ailments. One controversial condition is **chronic fatigue syndrome**. Called the "yuppie flu," chronic fatigue syndrome generally affects middle-class women, though men have also been diagnosed with it. Flu-like symptoms, including low-grade fever, sore throat, extreme fatigue, and emotional malaise, characterize the condition, which is often accompanied by depression. These symptoms may last for years and often result in disability. Sufferers experience difficulty in getting their condition recognized, not only by family and friends, but by insurance companies as well. Because of social hesitancy to accept chronic fatigue syndrome as legitimate, sufferers who are unable to work are often denied disability. Advocates have responded by renaming the disorder **chronic fatigue immuno-deficiency syndrome**. This renaming associates the disorder with more scientific, readily recognized diseases. More families, physicians, and employers are now taking the disease seriously, so chronic fatigue sufferers are gaining support.

People with mental illnesses equally struggle for recognition and understanding. Although treatment conditions and understanding of mental illness have drastically improved, critics and mental health providers argue that considerable work remains. Prior to the 1960s, most mentally ill patients were locked away in places referred to as "insane asylums," in which patients were often sedated for easy control. Because of new drugs that reduce or eliminate many symptoms and changed attitudes toward mental illness brought about by the work of sociologists and psychologists, many asylums closed and thousands of patients were released to community group homes, halfway houses, or independent living. This movement toward community care produced mixed results, with most mental health professionals concluding that the majority of deinstitutionalized patients adapt well with appropriate community placement and follow-up. Critics point to an increase in homelessness coinciding with deinstitutionalization. They claim many homeless are mentally ill patients who need institutionalization or at least better mental health care.

Communities now face a number of issues due to deinstitutionalization because many localities object to group homes and halfway houses being located in their communities. Many wrongly believe that the mentallly ill are more likely to commit crimes. Because of this misperception, as well as others, recovered mentally ill people, as well as those diagnosed and in treatment, are still stigmatized and discriminated against. In addition, turf wars can exist among mental-health professionals and over the use of drugs to control problematic behaviors. Psychiatrists and other medical doctors can prescribe drugs, while nonmedical professionals cannot. Insurance companies limit the kind of professional mentally ill patients may see and the length and cost of treatment. All these issues make it more difficult for mentally ill patients to get and remain in treatment.

Some mental illnesses, such as paranoid schizophrenia, require drug treatment for normal functioning. Patients in the community sometimes neglect to take their medication when they start feeling better, opting out of continued treatment and resulting in a relapse. Patients who stop taking their medications are the ones most likely to become homeless or to pose a danger to themselves or others. These are not the majority of patients being treated for a mental illness, however. People with conditions such as depression, panic, bipolar disorder (formerly known as manic depression), and a host of other debilitating conditions can respond well to other therapies in addition to medication. With treatment, they are no different from any other member of society. With increased awareness of mental and emotional disorders, finding cost-effective ways to meet society's need to appropriately care for these patients and benefit from their many talents will become more critical.

Major health problems in the United States

Over the 20th century, medicine responded to the most common health threats with effective treatments. By the end of the century, the leading causes of death had changed dramatically. According to the national Center for Health Statistics, the top ten causes of death are: heart disease, cancer, blood vessel diseases, accidents, lung diseases (not cancer), pneumonia and flu, diabetes, suicide, liver disease, and homicide. At the beginning of the century, the leading causes of death were tuberculosis, pneumonia, diarrhea, heart disease, nephritis, accidents, blood vessel diseases, cancer, bronchitis, and diphtheria.

Discovery and development of vaccines and antibiotics meant that diseases once deadly are curable or nonexistent. People live longer, thus suffering more diseases associated with old age such as heart disease, cancer, and blood vessel diseases. What has also changed is physicians' abilities to recognize and diagnose disease more accurately. In the past a death may have been ascribed to "old age," when today a physician might diagnose cancer.

What cannot be overlooked is the eleventh cause of death: AIDS, or acquired immune deficiency syndrome. First recognized in 1981, the origin of AIDS is still controversial, though many experts find evidence pointing to African monkeys. In the United States, the disease first appeared in male homosexuals. According to the Centers for Disease Control, the most common transmission of AIDS is through homosexual sex (52 percent). Other means of transmission are drug injection, 25 percent; heterosexual sex, 8 percent; homosexual sex and drug addiction, 7 percent; undetermined, 6 percent; and blood transfusions, 2 percent. The lengthy incubation period, sometimes lasting several years, contributes to its spread. While AIDS is the eleventh cause of death for the overall population, it is the leading cause of death for men age 24-44 in the United States.

Most common drugs: Alcohol and nicotine
The most commonly abused drugs in the United States are alcohol and nicotine. According to the statistical abstract, Americans consume on average 37 gallons of alcohol per year, the majority being beer at an average of 32 gallons per year. The remaining 5 gallons is comprised of 3 gallons of wine and 2 gallons of other distilled alcohol. At this rate, Americans consume more beer than either coffee or milk. Beer consumption has become a major issue on college campuses with recent epidemics of binge drinking, particularly by college males. Many incidents have resulted in injury and death. Although many recent studies have extolled the health benefits of moderate alcohol consumption, the emphasis of these studies is upon *moderate* consumption or one or fewer glasses of wine per day. Some emerging

studies indicate that the health benefits may be the same for grape juice and wine. Alcohol increases the risk of birth defects, and women who are or may become pregnant should not consume alcohol.

In 1964 the surgeon general issued the first warning that smoking could be hazardous to health. Since then the evidence has mounted and the powerful tobacco industry has increasingly found itself on the losing side of lawsuits. Emphysema, lung cancer, heart disease, and other cancers are attributed to smoking. Morbidity experts estimate nicotine kills about 390,000 Americans each year, making it the most deadly recreational drug. Individuals and states have sued for damages in these losses, and for the costs incurred with caring for nicotine-induced diseases. The role of second-hand smoke in disease has also been recognized. Although cigarette advertising is limited, it remains a central controversy, especially advertising aimed at teens and youth.

The Medical Establishment and Professions

Over the last 150 years, professionalism and delivery of health care have changed dramatically. Prior to the beginning of the 20th century, the sick could seek treatment from any number of sources besides physicians, including barbers, midwives, druggists, herb specialists, or even ministers. No standardized medical education system or licensing process existed, and no one oversaw the practices of anyone claiming to be a doctor. In many cases, becoming a doctor followed the same process as any other profession: apprenticeship to someone already a "doctor."

In 1847, the American Medical Association (AMA) was formed as a self-regulating body to set standards of professionalism and fight for a more scientific definition of medicine. At first, the organization exerted limited influence; however, as researchers identified bacteria and viruses as causes of disease and developed effective vaccines, its influence grew. The AMA also openly fought against alternative approaches to health care and certified only physicians who completed AMA-approved programs. The AMA expelled those who failed to complete such programs, or those who used alternative methods such as chiropractic or herbalism.

A definite turning point in medical care came in 1908 with the release of the **Flexner report**. Funded by the Carnegie Foundation for the Advancement of Teaching, Abraham Flexner investigated medical schools and declared only 82 of 160 acceptable. He cited problems such as inadequate materials, nonexistent libraries, and training programs of only two years. Flexner recommended that the "most promising" medical schools that had high standards of admission and training be supported with foundation and other philanthropic money. The best schools remained open, while the AMA forced the remainder to close. Thus, the Flexner report led to the professionalization of medicine. Physicians now had to undergo rigorous training, base their approach on theory, self-regulate, exercise authority over patients, and serve society.

The importance of the Flexner report was that for the first time it defined acceptable standards and pointed out inconsistencies and extreme deficiencies in medical education at the time. In some cases, folks could "buy" a medical degree by attending a diploma mill, and doctors improved their incomes by taking on more apprentices than they could actually teach.

While AMA supporters point to its role in protecting public interest and improving medical care, critics point to what they call the AMA's monopoly over medicine. The organization locked out those who did not adhere to the strict, narrow interpretations of the AMA. Interestingly, the medical schools closed by the Flexner report included all but two schools training blacks and one training women. Critics charge that the AMA became an all-powerful, white male organization that promoted a perception of doctors as all-knowing authority figures with power over nurses, midwives, and patients.

Doctors' use of technical language, confusing and intimidating to patients, reinforced their superiority, as they possessed the power to dispense or withhold information or treatment. Patient advocates argue, and substantial recent research supports the view that passive patients are likely to remain quiet, depriving the doctor of information that can alter a diagnosis. According to these critics, the hierarchy of medicine with doctors on top and everyone else at the bottom can negatively influence patient care.

Millions of Americans, disenchanted with or discouraged by traditional medicine, have returned to alternative forms of medicine. In recent years, naturopaths, herbalists, acupuncturists, and chiropractors have gained new clout and business. Each of these groups has also become more professional, regulating itself and setting standards. However, most alternative therapists work to avoid exerting too much authority over patients, aiming instead for partnership in treatment.

Chiropractors, who generally receive more training than most other practitioners of alternative medicine, have started to gain respect and recognition from the AMA. Many physicians practicing traditional medicine work cooperatively with alternative practitioners to treat patients. Others still openly oppose alternative medicine. Nevertheless, the current trend is for patients to seek greater control and understanding of their health care, demanding more information and choices in the process.

Health Care Availability: Costs and Inequality

No one denies that modern health care is expensive, but what factors contribute to the rising cost?

Of course, continually advancing technology provides the most obvious and perhaps greatest cause. Innovations in all forms of medical equipment, surgical techniques, and therapies are costly on their own, but also require specialists to operate them, or additional training for existing specialists. Patients, with more access to information about new technology through the Internet and other sources, expect the latest technology in their own treatment. Research and physician demands to use new techniques to explore all possibilities in patient care fuel this expectation.

The rising cost of physician care provides the next most significant contributor to rising medical costs. As technologies have increased so have the numbers of, types of, and demands for specialists. Specialists generally charge more for services than general practitioners, family practitioners, or internal medicine practitioners. Surgeons, radiologists, and endocrinologists earn as much as $80,000 more per year than a general practitioner. Cardiologists, gynecologists, and anesthesiologists earn approximately $30,000 more per year. Some specialists, such as pathologists, oncologists, and pediatricians, actually earn less than general practitioners. Even so, physicians, as a group, are in the top 1-percent income bracket, with incomes that consistently remain ahead of inflation.

Another contributor to rising health-care costs is malpractice insurance. From the 1980s to the 1990s, the cost of malpractice insurance doubled or tripled, depending upon the specialty, and most specialists pay higher rates.

The availability of newer, more expensive drugs, particularly newer antibiotics and drug treatments for AIDS patients, also contribute substantially to rising costs. Some of these medications may cost more than a hundred dollars for a single dose. The cost of medicine has become a public policy issue and a social problem as people forgo medication to pay for food and housing; this is especially true among those elderly who do not have prescription medicine coverage.

Managed Care as a Means of Cost Control

With health-care costs increasing, health insurance providers are looking for ways to reduce costs. Traditionally, patients paid for most medical care on a **fee-for-service** basis, where physicians, laboratories, and hospitals charged set fees for procedures. Patients either paid the fees directly or paid a partial fee with a private insurance company paying the remainder. The patient and his or her employer shared the cost of premium payments to the insurance company. Such systems do not typically cover serious illness, or if they do, insurance companies substantially raise premiums for the individual and the employer.

Until the last decade or so, most traditional insurance plans covered serious illness but not routine care. Blue Cross had separate plans for doctor visits and hospitalizations. In most plans, patients would pay the cost of check-ups and preventive testing. Insurance covered costs associated with a diagnosed illness and with hospitalization. "Gold-standard" plans, such as those held by the Auto Workers and Steel Workers, covered virtually everything. This system did not promote wellness, however, as many patients whose plans did not cover routine doctor visits and minor illnesses did not go for checkups and preventive tests. If you didn't have a lump, insurance did not pay for a mammogram; the patient did and the cost was prohibitive. But most people who had insurance were covered to some extent (mostly 80 percent insurance, 20 percent patient, until the patient reached a set limit).

HMOs were set up to approach health from a wellness perspective rather than a disease perspective. HMOs believed you could save money and lives by getting regular checkups and treating illnesses in their earliest stages, where the costs were lower and the prognoses better. Some argue that the current HMO system, which expects insurance to pay for wellness and illness, increases costs by encouraging visits for minor illnesses that a patient would forego if he had to pay the bill. Most hospitals at the time were nonprofit or not-for-profit, so the expectations of high profits based on holding down costs were not part of that system, though "profits" were indeed made. The requirements of remaining nonprofit funneled most of these profits into new programs or expanded facilities.

In response to this situation, managed care organizations emerged as nonprofit organizations to reduce health-care costs and provide broader coverage. **Managed care organizations** are groups of physicians, specialists, and often hospitals, coordinating with each other to provide care for a set monthly fee. These systems control the patient's access to doctors, specialists, laboratories, and treatment facilities. HMOs hire physicians as salaried employees rather than paying them on a fee-for-service basis. In this system, the medical clinics receive the same amount of money regardless of how frequently patients see the doctor. Because no connection exists between services rendered and fees paid, the incentive is to keep costs down. Critics of this system point out that business managers or non-medical personnel trying to hold down costs frequently overturn medical decisions made by doctors.

Although the number of HMOs has skyrocketed in the last few years, medical experts predict the decline if not the demise of HMOs because of the impact on patient care and widespread public dissatisfaction. HMOs are not traditionally considered managed care, and there are more managed care models than just HMOs, such as Preferred Provider Systems. Although begun as nonprofits, most managed care systems are for-profit, and many hospitals are now for-profit, introducing a strong profit-motive (not just a hold-down-costs motive) throughout the system. Members of managed care organizations can only visit approved doctors and stay at approved hospitals and get approved tests. They cannot see other doctors or even specialists within the managed care system without an okay from a primary care physician, who is incentivized not to make such recommendations. The blatant profit motive in many cases accounts for patient distrust of the system and dissatisfaction from everyone involved except for high-salaried system administrators and CEOs. Other issues include replacing highly trained nursing and physician staff with lesser trained assistants to save costs, overuse of emergency rooms, a growing shortage of hospital beds for critically ill patients, hospice and home health care, and the provision of follow-up social services to patients.

Access to Health Care

Discussion of fee-for-service or HMOs generally applies to middle-class employed persons. But what about the working poor, the unemployed, or the disabled? What options exist for them? Unfortunately, in the United States, access to health care is still closely tied to the ability to pay for such care, either personally or through insurance. Therefore, people who are not covered by health plans, are unemployed, or are disabled qualify for only limited access to health care. The United States, as one of the few Western nations without a national health care plan, falls far behind most other industrialized nations in providing care for such people. This fact is ironic considering that the United States spends more per person on health care than any other industrialized nation.

Without a doubt, the need for health care is significant, especially among the poor. Sociologists point to substantial evidence that shows the poor are sicker, die younger, and have higher infant mortality rates than the non-poor. Because minorities also tend to be poorer than non-minorities, poor-quality health care disproportionately affects them. Blacks have the highest death rate in the United States, followed by Hispanics. Whites have the lowest. Violence and accidents, both of whose rates are higher in the United States than in other industrialized nations, also contribute to high health costs.

The government tried to respond to the needs of the poor in the 1960s with Medicaid and Medicare. **Medicaid** is a federally funded program that provides medical insurance to the poor, disabled, and welfare recipients. Similarly, **Medicare** is a federally funded program that provides medical insurance for all people age 65 and older.

Although these programs have provided considerable benefits to many people, they have come under fire for a variety of reasons. Critics argue that the programs are too costly for the services provided, many are wasteful and inefficient, and, because of poor monitoring, these programs are often routinely abused by unscrupulous medical practitioners who defraud the system. To address billing fraud, the Office of the Inspector General (OIG) now aggressively investigates questionable billing to the Health Care and Finance Administration (HCFA), which oversees Medicare and Medicaid. The OIG expects all providers to implement and audit a **compliance plan**, that is, a comprehensive procedure and audit manual that demonstrates diligence in correct billing and avoidance of fraud. A new industry of consultants and legal advisors emerged during the 1990s and continue to assist practices with their compliance plans.

Recent political debates have sought to reform or abolish Medicare and Medicaid in their present forms or reduce the amounts paid for some procedures. Unfortunately, efforts to reduce Medicaid and Medicare costs may actually contribute to the overall rise in the cost of medical care. For example, many laboratory services are reimbursed at or below the cost to perform the test and produce the report. A laboratory processing a standard biopsy may break even or lose money depending on the complexity of the case. For every dollar lost on Medicare cases, the laboratory needs to make up that loss elsewhere. If Medicare or Medicaid were to pay less for these services, laboratories would be forced to charge more for tests to non-Medicare and Medicaid patients, refuse to accept Medicare and Medicaid tests, or go out of business. Also, there is a gap between where Medicaid ends and private insurance picks up. Many of the working poor are not covered by Medicaid, their companies do not provide health insurance, and they can't afford private insurance, so they are among the 40 to 60 million uninsured. Medicare is also facing problems as Medicare HMOs go out of business and doctors limit or refuse to accept patients covered by Medicare and Medicaid because of low payments, late payments, and excessive paperwork.

Euthanasia: The Right to Die?

While health and medicine usually look at improving and extending life, increasingly medical professionals and society are being forced to ask how far those efforts should go. Perhaps the most pressing ethical medical dilemma concerns whether an individual has the right to die. **Euthanasia**, or mercy killing, means the deliberate killing of a patient who is terminally ill and/or in severe and chronic pain. More recently, "physician-assisted suicide" has superseded the term euthanasia as terminally ill patients take more assertive roles in expressing their wishes and requesting physician support.

Although technology and advanced drugs provide physicians with "heroic" means of prolonging life, more people are questioning whether doing so is the right action, and, more importantly, many are asking why they must suffer at all with painful terminal diseases like Huntington's Disease, Alzheimer's, or the end-stages of AIDS. Those in favor of physician-assisted suicide argue that patients remain in control, administer the lethal drugs themselves, and die by choice with limited pain and suffering. Dr. Jack Kevorkian has stood at the center of the debate for providing lethal drugs to terminally ill or profoundly suffering patients who want to die. Despite arrests and jail sentences, Kevorkian continues to assist patients in their deaths.

Opponents to physician-assisted suicide point to several concerns:

- Making an accurate terminal diagnosis can be difficult because doctors do make mistakes and many patients beat the odds.

- Patients who claim they want physician-assisted suicide may be reasoning through the clouds of depression, which often triggers suicidal thoughts. Treat the depression, and the patient regains the will to live.

- Inadequate pain management often causes patients to long for death. Many people harshly criticize a medical establishment that they claim is insensitive to or outright fails to provide adequate pain management. In these cases, critics say, relieve the pain (even with addictive drugs) and many patients enjoy life again.

- Of greatest concern to opponents of physician-assisted suicide is the risk that the "right to die" could become the "responsibility to die." People may see poor or vulnerable individuals, especially the elderly, as a burden and pressure them into "doing their duty" of dying.

Overall, opponents feel that allowing physician-assisted suicide devalues human life and fails to address deeper issues in the society.

After protracted debate and two years of court challenges, the state of Oregon legalized physician-assisted suicide. A terminally ill patient must obtain a terminal diagnosis from at least two physicians who declare that the patient has six months or less to live. The patient must be evaluated for depression and meet other qualifications. If the request is approved, the patient must wait a minimum of two weeks before becoming eligible to receive the lethal prescription.

Although the physician-assisted suicide law has seen limited use since its implementation, it has had an unexpected consequence. The debate over the law has forced medical professionals to reevaluate pain treatment in Oregon. Physicians are more willing to prescribe pain medications, and the number and quality of hospice care facilities has rapidly increased. Harshest opponents of physician-assisted suicide admit there have been some positive outcomes from the Oregon experiment, although they still oppose the law, and the debate continues.

Humans throughout history have generally favored large families—for the most part to assure survival of a particular family line or racial group. High death rates from plagues, predators, and wars led people to produce as many offspring as possible. However, the situation has changed dramatically in the 20th century as technological advances of one sort or another have caused a global "population explosion," with the world currently gaining 90 million people each year (most of this increase in poorer countries). Given this trend, the global population will exceed 6 billion in the early 2000s, and 8 billion by the 2020s. Understandably, sociologists around the world exhibit urgent concern about increases in the global population.

Population

Demography (from the Greek word meaning "description of people") is the study of human populations. The discipline examines the size and composition of populations, as well as the movement of people from locale to locale. **Demographers** also analyze the effects of population growth and its control.

Several demographic variables play central roles in the study of human populations, especially *fertility* and *fecundity, mortality* and *life expectancy,* and *migration.*

Fertility and fecundity

A population's size is first affected by **fertility**, which refers to the number of children that an average woman bears during her reproductive years—from puberty to menopause. People sometimes confuse the term fertility with **fecundity**, which refers to the number of children an average woman is capable of bearing. Such factors as health, finances, and personal decision sharply affect fecundity.

To determine a country's fertility rate, demographers use governmental records to figure the **crude birth rate** (the number of live births for every thousand people in a population). They calculate this rate by dividing the number of live births in a year by the total population, and then multiplying the result by 1,000. As one might expect, the governmental records used in this type of research may not be completely accurate, especially in third-world countries where such records may not even exist.

While the world's average fertility rate is about 3 children per woman, its fecundity rate is about 20 per woman. The highest fertility rate (nearly 6 children per woman) in the world occurs in Africa, whereas the lowest occurs in Europe (about 1.5). The fertility rate for women in the United States is about 2.

Mortality and expectancy

Mortality, or the number of deaths in a society's population, also influences population size. Similar to the crude birth rate, demographers calculate the **crude death rate**, or the number of deaths annually per 1,000 people in the population. Demographers calculate this figure by dividing the number of deaths in a year by the total population, and then multiplying the result by 1,000. The crude death rate in the United States normally stays around 8 or 9.

Infant mortality rate, which is the number of deaths among infants under age one for each 1,000 live births in a year, provides demographers with another measure. Compared to other countries, North American infant mortality rates tend to be low. Still, the figures can vary considerably *within* a society. For example, African Americans have an infant mortality rate of about 19 compared to those of whites who have a rate of about 8.

A low infant mortality correlates with a higher **life expectancy**, which is the average lifespan of a society's population. U.S. males and females born today can look forward to living into their 70s, which exceeds the life expectancy of those in low-income countries by 20 years.

Migration

Finally, **migration** (the movement of people from one place to another) affects population size. While some migration is involuntary, such as when slaves where brought to America, other migration is voluntary, such as when families move from cities into suburbs.

Migration into an area, called **immigration**, is measured as the **immigration rate**, which is the number of people entering a region per each 1,000 people in the population. Migration out of an area, or **emigration**, is measured as the **emigration rate**, which is the number leaving per each 1,000 people in the population. **Internal migration** is the movement from one area to another within a country's borders.

Population growth

Fertility, mortality, and migration all influence the size of a society's population. Poorer countries tend to grow almost completely from internal causes (for example, high birth rates due to the absence of reliable contraception), while richer countries tend to grow from both internal causes and migration. Demographers determine a population's natural **growth rate** by subtracting the crude death rate from the crude birth rate. The world's low-growth nations tend to be more industrialized, such as the United States and Europe. The high-growth countries tend to be less industrialized, such as Africa and Latin America.

Population composition

Demographers also take an interest in the composition of a society's population. For example, they study the **gender ratio** (or **sex ratio**), which is the number of males per 100 females in a population. The sex ratio in the United States is about 93 males for every 100 females. In most areas of the world, the gender ratio is less than 100 because females normally outlive men. Yet in some cultures that practice female infanticide, such as among the Yanomamo, the ratio can reach well above 100.

Malthusian theory

The field of demography arose two centuries ago in response to the population growth of that day. **Thomas Robert Malthus** (1766-1834), English economist and clergyman, argued that increases in population, if left unchecked, would eventually result in social chaos. Malthus predicted that the human population would continue to increase *exponentially* (1, 2, 4, 16, 256 . . .) until the situation is out of control. He also warned that food production would only increase *arithmetically* (1, 2, 3, 4, 5 . . .) because of limitations in available farmland. To say the least, Malthus provided a disturbing vision of the future that included massive, global starvation as a consequence of unrestrained population growth.

As it turned out, Malthus' predictions were mistaken because he failed to account for technological advancements and ingenuity that would increase agricultural and farm production, not to mention the increasing development and acceptance of birth control methods. Yet Malthus' forebodings do not lack merit. As noted by the New Malthusians, a group of demographers, assets such as habitable and fertile land, clean air, and fresh water are finite resources. And with medical advances increasing fertility and lowering death rates, the global population continues to grow exponentially with no end in sight.

Demographic transition theory

Replacing Malthus' ideas today, **demographic transition theory** defines population growth in an alternating pattern of stability, rapid growth, and then stability again. This theory proposes a three-stage model of growth.

- **Stage 1: Stable population growth.** In this stage, birth and death rates roughly balance each other. Most societies throughout history have stayed at this stage.

- **Stage 2: Rapid population growth.** Death rates fall sharply while birth rates remain high in Stage 2. Most poor countries today fit into this stage. Malthus formed his ideas during one such high-growth period.

- **Stage 3: Stable population growth.** In this stage, fertility falls because high living standards make raising children expensive. Women working outside the home also favor smaller families, brought about by widespread use of birth control. Death rates drop because of technological advances in medicine. With low birth rates and death rates, the population only grows slowly, if at all. It may, in fact, witness **population shrinkage**, in which deaths outnumber births in a society.

Stage 3 suggests that technology holds the key to population control. Instead of the out-of-control population explosions that Malthus predicted, demographic transition theory claims that technology will ultimately control population growth and ensure enough food for all.

Population control: The importance of family planning

Historically, many groups and societies have discouraged **contraception** (the prevention of conception, or birth control) to assure survival of its members and humanity as a whole. Certain religious groups strongly disapprove of sexual activity that does not culminate in coitus and the possibility of conception. Other groups place little importance on the matter of contraception. The Yanomamo of South America, for instance, harbor little or no concept of contraception. Instead, they parent as many children as possible, and then kill off those they view as the undesirable, such as some females and deformed infants.

Modern medicine has spread throughout different parts of the world, and people of all ages now live longer, causing the world's population to explode in growth. In fact, at five billion today, the world's population doubles, on average, every 35 years, with most of this growth occurring in developing countries. Given this population crisis, certain governments, like that of China, regulate the number of births allowed per household.

Besides the issue of controlling overpopulation, other benefits to practicing contraception exist. For example, a young couple may want to postpone having children until their finances improve. Or an unmarried, sexually active teenager may wish to finish her education or get married before starting a family, thereby reducing her chances of eventually relying on the government for financial support.

Family planning also plays an important role in protecting the physical health of both mother and child. The older or younger a woman is, and the closer together she bears children (that is, more frequently than every two years), the greater the risk of pregnancy and birth complications, early infant mortality, and maternal death. For example, women over age 40 or under age 19 have an increased risk of bearing a child of low birth weight, and thus a variety of birth defects and even outright death. Estimates say that approximately one million teenage women in the United States become pregnant each year.

Urbanization

By the early 1900s both Great Britain and the United States had become predominantly urbanized nations; since that time, urbanization has been occurring around the globe at a rapid rate. Today, as many as 50 percent of the world's population lives in urban areas, compared to only a few percent just 200 years ago.

Sociologists studying urbanization trends note three distinct historical stages in the development of cities: *preindustrial, industrial,* and *metropolitan-megalopolitan* stages.

Preindustrial cities

For the vast majority of human history, as far as anyone knows, people roamed about in search of sustenance. While they gathered edible plants, fished, and hunted, our ancestors could never find enough food in one area to sustain themselves for an extended period of time. Consequently, they had to keep moving until they could find another place in which to settle temporarily.

Eventual technological improvements—such as simple tools and information on how to farm and raise animals—allowed people to settle in one place. They built villages, with perhaps only a few hundred people living in each, and, for the following 5,000 years, produced just enough food for themselves—with nothing more in reserve.

About 5,000 years ago, however, humans developed such innovations as irrigation, metallurgy, and animal-drawn plows. These developments allowed farmers to produce an excess of food beyond their immediate needs. The resulting surplus of food led some people to make their living in other ways: for instance, by making pottery, weaving, and engaging in other nonagricultural activities that they could sell or exchange with others for the surplus food. As a result, people moved off the farms, commerce developed, and cities began to form.

Preindustrial cities—which first arose on fertile lands along rivers in the Middle East, Egypt, and China—were quite small compared to today's cities. Most preindustrial cities housed fewer than 10,000 inhabitants. Others, like Rome, may have contained as many as several hundred thousand people.

Preindustrial cities differed significantly from today's cities. The residential and commercial districts were not as sharply separated as they are today. Most traders and artisans worked at home, although people with the same trades tended to live in the same areas of town. People in cities also segregated themselves from one another according to class, ethnicity, and religion—with little or no chance for social mobility or interaction with other groups.

Industrial cities

Between 1700 and 1900, increasing numbers of people moved into cities, resulting in an **urban revolution**. For example, in 1700 less than 2 percent of British people lived in cities, but by 1900 the majority of them did so. The United States and other European countries soon attained similar levels of urbanization, driven by the *Industrial Revolution*.

Industrialization produced the mechanization of agriculture, which, in turn, limited the amount of work available on farms. This lack of employment forced farm laborers to move to cities to find work. This migration of workers from rural to urban areas then gave rise to the **industrial city**.

The industrial city was larger, more densely populated, and more diverse than its preindustrial counterpart. It contained many people of varying backgrounds, interests, and skills who lived and worked together in a defined amount of space. The industrial city also served as a commercial center, supporting many businesses and factories.

The latter attracted large numbers of immigrants from other countries hoping to better themselves by securing stable work and finding a "fresh start."

Metropolis and megalopolis cities

As larger and larger industrial cities spread outward in the early 1900s, they formed **metropolises** (large cities that include surrounding *suburbs,* which are lands outside the city limits, usually with separate governance). While some suburbs become distinct cities in and of themselves, they retain strong geographic, economic, and cultural ties to their "parent" city. Many metropolitan areas house a million or more residents.

The upper and middle classes ultimately brought about the so-called flight to the suburbs. As economic woes increasingly plagued cities in the latter half of the 1900s, many families decided to move out of their inner-city neighborhoods and into the suburbs. The ability to afford an automobile also influenced this migration. Beginning in the 1970s, most suburbs were largely "bedroom communities," which means that suburban residents commuted into the city to work and shop, and then returned to the suburb at night. Commuting presented a downside, but most people felt that escaping "urban ghettoization," or the tendency for the quality of life in inner cities to decline, was well worth any hassles, given the fact that suburbs tended to offer nicer and larger homes, better schools, less crime, and less pollution than cities provided.

Today, suburbs continue to grow and develop. Many have become economic centers in their own right. Offices, hospitals, and factories coexist with shopping malls, sports complexes, and housing subdivisions. In this way, many suburbs have essentially become small (and, in some cases, not so small) cities. Demographically, suburbs tend to attract "whiter" and more affluent residents than do cities. Yet not all suburbs and *suburbanites* are alike. Even within a suburb, families of varying ethnic and religious backgrounds exist.

Because of all this growth, many suburbs have developed "urban" problems, such as air and water pollution, traffic congestion, and gangs. To escape these problems, some people have chosen to move to rural areas. Others have chosen to return to and revive their cities by renovating and remodeling buildings and neighborhoods. Such an interest in **urban renewal** (also called *gentrification*) has turned some slums into decent areas in which to live, work, and raise a family.

The vast urban complex known as a **megalopolis** was created as suburbs continued to grow and merge with other suburbs and metropolitan areas. That is, some suburbs and cities have grown so large that they end up merging with other suburbs and cities, forming a virtually continuous region. One example of a megalopolis is the hundreds of miles of almost uninterrupted urbanization from Boston to Washington, D.C. The typical megalopolis consists of literally millions of people.

CHAPTER 16
CONTEMPORARY MASS MEDIA

Mass media is communication—whether written, broadcast, or spoken—that reaches a large audience. This includes television, radio, advertising, movies, the Internet, newspapers, magazines, and so forth.

The Role and Influence of Mass Media

Mass media is a significant force in modern culture, particularly in America. Sociologists refer to this as a **mediated culture** where media reflects and creates the culture. Communities and individuals are bombarded constantly with messages from a multitude of sources including TV, billboards, and magazines, to name a few. These messages promote not only products, but moods, attitudes, and a sense of what is and is not important. Mass media makes possible the concept of celebrity: without the ability of movies, magazines, and news media to reach across thousands of miles, people could not become famous. In fact, only political and business leaders, as well as the few notorious outlaws, were famous in the past. Only in recent times have actors, singers, and other social elites become celebrities or "stars."

The current level of media saturation has not always existed. As recently as the 1960s and 1970s, television, for example, consisted of primarily three networks, public broadcasting, and a few local independent stations. These channels aimed their programming primarily at two-parent, middle-class families. Even so, some middle-class households did not even own a television. Today, one can find a television in the poorest of homes, and multiple TVs in most middle-class homes. Not only has availability increased, but programming is increasingly diverse with shows aimed to please all ages, incomes, backgrounds, and attitudes. This widespread availability and exposure

makes television the primary focus of most mass-media discussions. More recently, the Internet has increased its role exponentially as more businesses and households "sign on." Although TV and the Internet have dominated the mass media, movies and magazines—particularly those lining the aisles at grocery checkout stands—also play a powerful role in culture, as do other forms of media.

What role does mass media play? Legislatures, media executives, local school officials, and sociologists have all debated this controversial question. While opinions vary as to the extent and type of influence the mass media wields, all sides agree that mass media is a permanent part of modern culture. Three main sociological perspectives on the role of media exist: the limited-effects theory, the class-dominant theory, and the culturalist theory.

Limited-effects theory

The **limited-effects theory** argues that because people generally choose what to watch or read based on what they already believe, media exerts a negligible influence. This theory originated and was tested in the 1940s and 1950s. Studies that examined the ability of media to influence voting found that well-informed people relied more on personal experience, prior knowledge, and their own reasoning. However, media "experts" more likely swayed those who were less informed. Critics point to two problems with this perspective. First, they claim that limited-effects theory ignores the media's role in framing and limiting the discussion and debate of issues. How media frames the debate and what questions members of the media ask change the outcome of the discussion and the possible conclusions people may draw. Second, this theory came into existence when the availability and dominance of media was far less widespread.

Class-dominant theory

The **class-dominant theory** argues that the media reflects and projects the view of a minority elite, which controls it. Those people who own and control the corporations that produce media comprise this elite. Advocates of this view concern themselves particularly with massive corporate mergers of media organizations, which limit competition and put big business at the reins of media—especially news media. Their concern is that when ownership is restricted, a few people then have the ability to manipulate what people can see or hear. For example, owners can easily avoid or silence stories that expose unethical corporate behavior or hold corporations responsible for their actions.

The issue of sponsorship adds to this problem. Advertising dollars fund most media. Networks aim programming at the largest possible audience because the broader the appeal, the greater the potential purchasing audience and the easier selling air time to advertisers becomes. Thus, news organizations may shy away from negative stories about corporations (especially parent corporations) that finance large advertising campaigns in their newspaper or on their stations. Television networks receiving millions of dollars in advertising from companies like Nike and other textile manufacturers were slow to run stories on their news shows about possible human-rights violations by these companies in foreign countries. Media watchers identify the same problem at the local level where city newspapers will not give new cars poor reviews or run stories on selling a home without an agent because the majority of their funding comes from auto and real estate advertising. This influence also extends to programming. In the 1990s a network cancelled a short-run drama with clear religious sentiments, *Christy,* because, although highly popular and beloved in rural America, the program did not rate well among young city dwellers that advertisers were targeting in ads.

Critics of this theory counter these arguments by saying that local control of news media largely lies beyond the reach of large corporate offices elsewhere, and that the quality of news depends upon good journalists. They contend that those less powerful and not in

control of media have often received full media coverage and subsequent support. As examples they name numerous environmental causes, the anti-nuclear movement, the anti-Vietnam movement, and the pro-Gulf War movement.

While most people argue that a corporate elite controls media, a variation on this approach argues that a politically "liberal" elite controls media. They point to the fact that journalists, being more highly educated than the general population, hold more liberal political views, consider themselves "left of center," and are more likely to register as Democrats. They further point to examples from the media itself and the statistical reality that the media more often labels conservative commentators or politicians as "conservative" than liberals as "liberal."

Media language can be revealing, too. Media uses the terms "arch" or "ultra" conservative, but rarely or never the terms "arch" or "ultra" liberal. Those who argue that a political elite controls media also point out that the movements that have gained media attention—the environment, anti-nuclear, and anti-Vietnam—generally support liberal political issucs. Predominantly conservative political issues have yet to gain prominent media attention, or have been opposed by the media. Advocates of this view point to the Strategic Arms Initiative of the 1980s Reagan administration. Media quickly characterized the defense program as "Star Wars," linking it to an expensive fantasy. The public failed to support it, and the program did not get funding or congressional support.

Culturalist theory
The **culturalist theory**, developed in the 1980s and 1990s, combines the other two theories and claims that people interact with media to create their own meanings out of the images and messages they receive. This theory sees audiences as playing an active rather than passive role in relation to mass media. One strand of research focuses on the audiences and how they interact with media; the other strand of research focuses on those who produce the media, particularly the news.

Theorists emphasize that audiences choose what to watch among a wide range of options, choose how much to watch, and may choose the mute button or the VCR remote over the programming selected by the network or cable station. Studies of mass media done by sociologists parallel text-reading and interpretation research completed by linguists (people who study language). Both groups of researchers find that when people approach material, whether written text or media images and messages, they interpret that material based on their own knowledge and experience. Thus, when researchers ask different groups to explain the meaning of a particular song or video, the groups produce widely divergent interpretations based on age, gender, race, ethnicity, and religious background. Therefore, culturalist theorists claim that, while a few elite in large corporations may exert significant control over what information media produces and distributes, personal perspective plays a more powerful role in how the audience members interpret those messages.

Creating News and Culture

Much of the sociological perspective about how news is created comes from researchers with the culturalist theory perspective. Journalists themselves also remain keenly aware of these issues and carefully study them. The central problem comes from the fact that many more events occur than the media can ever report on. Journalists must look at all the information and events before them and make decisions about what they report and what they do not. Because newspapers go to press on strict deadlines to be delivered on time, and because news shows must air live at regular times, deadlines in the news business are absolute. This situation forces reporters and news editors to make difficult decisions under pressure and with limited time.

Journalists also face competition to sell their news product. Newspapers run stories with the widest appeal to sell more papers and to draw more advertising. Television, and increasingly Internet news sites, compete to draw advertisers as well, and again, must frame their news to address the needs, interests, tastes, and appeal of the audience. As journalists make decisions about what to include and exclude, they are making choices about what is newsworthy, and, in fact, what is news. If reporters and editors do not deem information or an event as "newsworthy," then they do not report it, and it does not "become" news. In other words, journalists and media critics alike recognize that news reporters do as much to create the news as they do to report it, which means they also create reality as they report it. Even though reporters may report "only the facts," the facts that they select to report create a reality that audiences then interpret based on their own perceptions.

A principle espoused by many media experts adds to these issues. These experts argue that the form of communication (the medium used) plays a role in what kind of information journalists select. For example, a newspaper journalist's medium differs significantly from a television journalist's medium. Whereas newspapers emphasize the written word, television relies upon visual images, which means that events or information that can be conveyed through visual images are routinely presented while more verbal information or events receive little or no airtime.

Critics refer to this as a *tyranny of the image.* They point to the shift in television news reporting that has taken place from the 1950s and 1960s to the 1990s. During the earlier decades, 15-minute news broadcasts focused almost exclusively upon business and politics. Today, local newscasts can range anywhere from 30 to 90 minutes, and although the evening news includes some business and political reporting, crime and disasters overwhelm the airwaves. News has shifted from reporting information to telling stories: The news covers information and events that have clear plot lines or riveting drama because these stories play well with visual images. Static analyses of economic or business trends do not have the same dramatic appeal and rarely appear on network or local TV news, even though such information may impact the audience to a greater degree.

Experts worry that too much reliance on visual images and television will distort reality and prevent the adequate reporting of vital information. They look in particular at economic news, which affects all people. The news generally confines such information to the stock market results and a few other key statistics, which it fails to fully explain or put into context.

Political and economic events are frequently reported through the eyes of one person, whose touching and sometimes uncommon experience then becomes the image of the results of a real or proposed policy regardless of that policy's other effects, which may be more positive or negative. People relate to people, and almost all television news stories including politics and governmental actions seek out a "people angle," whether the people interviewed understand the issues involved or have any decision-making power.

Defenders of televised news respond that the visual images in many cases recount events more accurately and more objectively than verbal communication. In addition, defenders note that unless people choose to read or watch news stories, the news will not get out, no matter how well it's covered. If the news is not relevant, interesting, and visual, people won't turn to it and newscasters may soon have no influence at all. Newspeople say that their process is now more democratic, giving people what market research shows that people want rather than making "elitist" decisions about what people "should" or "need to" know.

Oversimplification and Stereotyping

All forms of mass media face tight restrictions on time and space. Newspapers and magazines have limits on column inches, while prime-time shows and news coverage have limited minutes. To cover many topics and issues, or to entertain, media generally simplifies stories or reduces them to fit in the allotted space or time. The goal is to make information and entertainment faster and more digestible for an audience. While this may lead to convenience for consumers, sociologists recognize that media frequently oversimplifies crucial social issues and other concerns.

Oversimplification, in turn, leads to stereotyping. Critics have targeted prime-time entertainment in particular for portraying distorted images of minorities and women. Although prime-time programming has increased the numbers and types of roles for minorities and women, programming as a whole still does not reflect the demographics of the general population. Prime-time programming remains whiter and younger than the average American population.

Some people are concerned that, as people pick and choose from so many sources and markets fragment, with young people watching young people shows and older people watching older people shows—and never the twain shall meet—there is no longer any truly "mass" media. As a result, Americans' common imagery and frame of reference for many issues is disappearing. Ignoring cultures and opinions different from one's own is now easier than ever, and critics fear that the eventual result may be less, rather than more, social cohesion.

Violence and Pornography in the Media

Most controversial of all topics in mass media is its role in violence and pornography through proliferation of programming with violent themes and action and overt sexual content.

Violence in the media

Researchers in each of the last three decades have produced major research studies on the role of media violence, especially its influence on children and adolescents. In 1972, the U.S. Surgeon General commissioned a study, which was followed in 1982 by a comprehensive study from the National Institute of Mental Health. Ten years later the American Psychological Association concluded its research. These three diverse groups with varying approaches and perspectives evaluated all available information. All three concluded, without reservation, that mass-media violence does indeed contribute to violence in people regardless of age, gender, race, or ethnicity. According to these studies, the primary danger lies in the fact that the media portrays violence as normal or acceptable, and the problem is compounded when the aggressor goes unpunished. Such portrayals lead to desensitization and a greater likelihood of aggressive behavior.

Pornography

Research into the effects of sexual materials is not as clear. Researchers distinguish between erotica, which is intended to be sexually stimulating but not demeaning, and pornography,which is intended to be sexually demeaning. They further note that both erotica and pornograhy can either be "softcore" (indirect in its display of sexual activity and the genitals) or "hardcore" (direct in its display of sexual activity and the genitals).

Numerous studies have been conducted to determine the effects of sexual materials on viewers and readers. To date—at least when discussing mutually consensual, softcore, nonviolent erotica and pornography—little evidence proves either negative or positive effects. However, violent pornography that depicts women in a degrading, humiliating, or demeaning manner may have different, more negative effects in terms of domestic violence, rape, and sexual harassment. The topic of the effects of pornography is controversial and hotly debated, and many experts call for more research in this area.

In the late 1960s, the U.S. Congress and President Lyndon B. Johnson formed the Commission on Obscenity and Pornography. Their 1970 report concluded that pornography was basically harmless. Although the commission confirmed that erotica and pornography sexually aroused both men and women, they also noted that it did not affect their general behavior, particularly in negative ways. Critics of the Johnson Commission report point out that the types of violent pornography so common today were uncommon when the commission gathered its information.

Not until the early to mid-1980s did evidence begin to mount suggesting that pornography negatively affects some men. Researchers found that certain men likely exhibit aggressive behavior and attitudes toward women after viewing violent pornography. This especially holds true for materials that picture women enjoying being raped, even though they may have initially resisted.

During the Reagan administration, the United States Attorney General's Commission on Pornography, more commonly remembered as the Meese Commission (named after Edwin Meese, Attorney General at the time), arrived at conclusions surprisingly different from the 1970 governmental study. The Meese Commission claimed a causal link between violent pornography and sexual violence toward women. They based their report on a review of a large collection of pornography in various forms and listening to the views of numerous experts, victims, and judges. Based on this assertion, the commission made nearly 100 recommendations designed to curb the dissemination of pornographic materials.

In response to the commission's conclusions, social scientists pointed out that what the research showed was not that exposure to aggressive/violent pornography affects sexual behavior per se, but that it affects aggressive behavior, a theory borne out by other studies involving nonsexual aggressive behavior.

More-recent research has much to say concerning what happens when adults watch or read violent pornographic materials—mainly, that sex and violence present a particularly harmful mix. Viewing such materials can increase males' acceptance of sexual and other types of aggression toward females. Males who have viewed violent pornography are also more likely to believe such myths as that women like being sexually overpowered or raped, "no" really means "yes," rape victims' injuries are not severe, or wife-battering is acceptable. Further, pornographers rarely depict sexual aggressors and perpetrators negatively, or show them being punished for their sexual aggression.

Social change refers to any significant alteration over time in behavior patterns and cultural values and norms. By "significant" alteration, sociologists mean changes yielding *profound* social consequences. Examples of significant social changes having long-term effects include the industrial revolution, the abolition of slavery, and the feminist movement.

Today's sociologists readily acknowledge the vital role that *social movements* play in inspiring discontented members of a society to bring about social change. Efforts to understand the nature of long-term social change, including looking for patterns and causes, has led sociologists to propose the evolutionary, functionalist, and conflict theories of change (discussed in the next few sections). All theories of social change also admit the likelihood of resistance to change, especially when people with vested interests feel unsettled and threatened by potential changes.

Social Movements

While technology, population, environment factors, and racial inequality can prompt social change, only when members of a society organize into social movements does true social change occur. The phrase **social movements** refers to collective activities designed to bring about or resist primary changes in an existing society or group.

Wherever they occur, social movements can dramatically shape the direction of society. When individuals and groups of people—civil rights activists and other visionaries, for instance—transcend traditional bounds, they may bring about major shifts in social policy and structures.

Even when they prove initially unsuccessful, social movements do affect public opinion. In her day, people considered Margaret Sanger's efforts to make birth control available extreme and even immoral, yet today in the United States, one can easily purchase contraceptive products.

Social scientists interest themselves in why social movements emerge. Do feelings of discontent, desires for a "change of pace," or even yearnings for "change for the sake of change" cause these shifts? Sociologists use two theories to explain why people mobilize for change: *relative deprivation* and *resource mobilization.*

Relative deprivation

When members of a society become dissatisfied or frustrated with their social, economic, and political situation, they yearn for changes. Social scientists have long noted that the actual conditions that people live under may not be at fault, but people's *perceptions* of their conditions are. **Relative deprivation** refers to the negative perception that differences exist between wants and actualities. In other words, people may not actually be deprived when they believe they are. A relatively deprived group is disgruntled because they feel less entitled or privileged than a particular reference group. For example, a middle-class family may feel relatively deprived when they compare their house to that of their upper-class physician.

For social discontent to translate into social movement, members of the society must feel that they deserve, or have a right to, more wealth, power, or status than they have. The dissatisfied group must also conclude that it cannot attain its goals via conventional methods, whether or not this is the case. The group will organize into a social movement only if it feels that collective action will help its cause.

The relative-deprivation theory takes criticism from a couple of different angles. First, some sociologists note that feelings of deprivation do not necessarily prompt people into acting. Nor must people feel deprived before acting. Moreover, this theory does not address why perceptions of personal or group deprivation cause some people to reform society, and why other perceptions do not.

Resource mobilization

Resource mobilization deals with how social movements mobilize resources: political pull, mass media, personnel, money, and so forth. A particular movement's effectiveness and success largely depends on how well it uses its resources.

Members of a social movement normally follow a charismatic leader, who mobilizes people for a cause. Charisma can fade, and many social movements collapse when this happens. Other movements, such as bureaucratic ones, manage to last, however, usually because they are highly organized.

Norms of behavior develop as people become part of a social movement. The movement may require its members to dress in special ways, boycott certain products, pay dues, attend marches or rallies, recruit new members, and use new language. Concerning the latter, recent social movements have given rise to new terms like *Hispanic American, African American, feminists,* and *psychiatrically disabled.*

For a social movement to succeed, leaders must heighten their followers' awareness of oppression. To stimulate their social movement in the 1960s and 1970s, feminists convinced women that they were being discriminated against in various arenas, including work, school, and home.

Unlike the relative-deprivation theory, the resource-mobilization theory emphasizes the strategic problems faced by social movements. Specifically, any movement designed to stimulate fundamental changes will surely face resistance to its activities. Critics feel the theory does not adequately discuss the issue of how opposition influences the actions and direction of social movements.

Models of Social Change

In their search to explain social change, sociologists sometimes examine historical data to better understand current changes and movements. They also rely on three basic theories of social change: *evolutionary, functionalist,* and *conflict* theories.

Evolutionary theory

Sociologists in the 19th century applied Charles Darwin's (1809-1882) work in biological evolution to theories of social change. According to **evolutionary theory**, society moves in specific directions. Therefore, early social evolutionists saw society as progressing to higher and higher levels. As a result, they concluded that their own cultural attitudes and behaviors were more advanced than those of earlier societies.

Identified in Chapter 1 as the "father of sociology," Auguste Comte subscribed to social evolution. He saw human societies as progressing into using scientific methods. Likewise, Emile Durkheim, one of the founders of functionalism, saw societies as moving from simple to complex social structures. Herbert Spencer compared society to a living organism with interrelated parts moving toward a common end. In short, Comte, Durkheim, and Spencer proposed **unilinear evolutionary theories**, which maintain that all societies pass through the same sequence of stages of evolution to reach the same destiny.

Contemporary social evolutionists like Gerhard Lenski, Jr., however, view social change as multilinear rather than unilinear. **Multilinear evolutionary theory** holds that change can occur in several ways and does not inevitably lead in the same direction. Multilinear theorists observe that human societies have evolved along differing lines.

Functionalist theory

Functionalist sociologists emphasize what maintains society, not what changes it. Although functionalists may at first appear to have little to say about social change, sociologist Talcott Parsons holds otherwise. Parsons (1902–1979), a leading functionalist, saw society in its natural state as being stable and balanced. That is, society naturally moves toward a state of *homeostasis*. To Parsons, significant social problems, such as union strikes, represent nothing but temporary rifts in the social order. According to his **equilibrium theory**, changes in one aspect of society require adjustments in other aspects. When these adjustments do not occur, equilibrium disappears, threatening social order. Parsons' equilibrium theory incorporates the evolutionary concept of continuing progress, but the predominant theme is stability and balance.

Critics argue that functionalists minimize the effects of change because all aspects of society contribute in some way to society's overall health. They also argue that functionalists ignore the use of force by society's powerful to maintain an illusion of stability and integration.

Conflict theory

Conflict theorists maintain that, because a society's wealthy and powerful ensure the status quo in which social practices and institutions favorable to them continue, change plays a vital role in remedying social inequalities and injustices.

Although Karl Marx accepted the evolutionary argument that societies develop along a specific direction, he did not agree that each successive stage presents an improvement over the previous stage. Marx noted that history proceeds in stages in which the rich always exploit the poor and weak as a class of people. Slaves in ancient Rome and the working classes of today share the same basic exploitation. Only by socialist revolution led by the proletariat (working class), explained Marx in his 1867 *Das Kapital,* will any society move into its final stage of development: a free, classless, and communist society.

Marx's view of social change is proactive; it does not rely on people remaining passive in response to exploitation or other problems in material culture. Instead, it presents tools for individuals wishing to take control and regain their freedom. Unlike functionalism and its emphasis on stability, Marx holds that conflict is desirable and needed to initiate social change and rid society of inequality.

Critics of Marx note that conflict theorists do not always realize that social upheaval does not inevitably lead to positive or expected outcomes.

Technology and Social Change

Technology is the application of scientific knowledge to the making of tools to solve specific problems. Technological advances such as automobiles, airplanes, radio, television, cellular phones, computers, modems, and fax machines have brought major advances and changes to the world. Indeed, 20th century technology has completely—and irreversibly—changed the way people meet, interact, learn, work, play, travel, worship, and do business.

Technological information increases exponentially: The entire database of scientific knowledge doubles every several years. This "technological explosion" is due in part to an "Information explosion," as well as to advances in storage, retrieval, and communication of data. In other words, a cycle occurs: Improvements in technology lead to increases in knowledge and information and, thus, to uncovering the means to create better technology. Consequently, sociologists are concerned with how technological societies will be forced to adapt to the social changes that improvements in technology will continue to bring.

Computer technology

In the 1990s, people witnessed an explosion of computer technology—both in America and around the globe, which has in turn led to a change in how and where people work. **Telecommuters** are employees of agencies or business firms who work full-time or part-time at home instead of in the office. They connect to their offices via electronic networking: phone, computer, e-mail, and fax. Telecommuting allows employees to work under supervisors in another state or country. This form of employment especially helps disabled individuals who are unable to leave home or travel to an office, as well as working parents of young children.

The Internet—the world's largest computer network—has revolutionized electronic networking. The number of people using the Internet continues to double annually, with at least 50 percent of all Americans "online" in 2000.

The Internet originally developed from a system built by the U.S. Defense Department to permit governmental work in the aftermath of a nuclear attack. Although originally only those with governmental or university positions could access the Internet, now virtually any home can purchase World Wide Web service. Net-surfers can telecommute, read articles, check stock prices, conduct research, comparison price, shop from home, meet others in chat rooms or on bulletin boards, take college courses, and even earn an accredited degree.

The Internet has certainly provided exciting new possibilities for electronic communication, yet critics argue that a dark side exists to this informational tool. One area of special concern, especially for families with young children, is the ability to access and download pornographic materials. Internet users can download pornographic photos, trade sexual messages on a bulletin board, have overtly sexual conversations with a distant "playmate," play erotic games, or purchase tickets for a singles cruise. In recent years, sexual predators have also used the Internet to identify potential victims. Other areas of concern include potential social isolation, random and reckless dissemination of nonverifiable or inaccurate information, plagiarism, and family estrangement.

Biotechnology

Recent decades have produced dramatic—though controversial—scientific advances in **biotechnology** (the application of technology to the practice of medicine). Advances in such areas as reproductive technologies, surrogate parenthood, sex preselection, and genetic engineering have raised difficult political, ethical, and moral questions.

Reproductive technologies and sex preselection

Not every couple wanting to conceive can do so. If they fail to conceive after one year or more of trying, the couple is considered infertile. At any one time, up to 20 percent of couples in the United States may be infertile.

In many cases, doctors can successfully treat infertility:

- **Fertility drugs** (ovulation-stimulating hormones) can help when the woman's inability to ovulate causes the infertility.

- **Artificial insemination**, which involves collecting and introducing sperm into the vagina using a syringe, proves particularly useful when the man possesses a below-normal sperm count.

- **In vitro fertilization**, or the "test-tube baby" method, involves fertilizing an egg outside the woman's body and implanting it into the uterus. This procedure is useful when the woman has blocked fallopian tubes.

- **Gamete intrafallopian transfer** ("GIFT") involves taking eggs from the woman's ovaries, mixing them with the man's sperm, and then inserting them into the fallopian tube. In this procedure, fertilization takes place inside the woman's body rather than outside. To date, couples in the United States have produced over 20,000 babies using alternatives such as these.

Some couples or individuals decide that adopting a child represents the best way of dealing with infertility. Others elect to utilize the services of a **surrogate mother**—a woman who contracts with a couple to carry their fetus to full term, deliver it, and adopt it to the couple. A physician may artificially inseminate the surrogate with the man's sperm or implant an in vitro fertilized egg into her uterus. Either way, the procedure remains controversial, given the many potential ethical, legal, and moral issues it raises. For example, questions of legal, moral, and biological parenthood can give rise to long and complicated custody proceedings.

Similar to surrogate motherhood, and also controversial, is **carrier implantation**. The procedure involves implanting a fertilized egg into a relative's uterus. Because a relative carries the fetus to term, the woman or couple avoids the expense and hassle of hiring a surrogate mother. Physicians have now successfully implanted embryos into women in their 50s, following hormone therapy to reverse the effects of menopause.

Sex preselection techniques designed to help a couple choose the gender of their unborn child have also proven controversial. Because sperm bearing the Y chromosome produce males, couples wanting a male baby attempt to increase the chances of a Y-bearing sperm fusing with the X-ovum. A number of sperm-separating techniques supposedly accomplish this. For example, doctors can impregnate the mother-to-be via artificial insemination of primarily Y-bearing sperm, which they have separated in a test tube. Success rates of sperm-separating techniques are questionable, with reported figures approaching 85 percent. Critics note that society cannot know the effects of gender imbalances created through sex preselection. Will people prefer more girls than boys? What happens to the future of marriage and family?

Genetic engineering

Perhaps even more presumptuous (or alarming, according to some critics) than reproductive technologies and sex preselection is altering human behavior through genetic engineering. **Cloning**, or the creation of exact replicas from a single genetic ancestor, represents the most extreme form of genetic engineering. Geneticists have cloned animals for years, but may soon focus their efforts on human beings.

One of the latest advances in genetic engineering is **gene therapy**, in which genetic engineers, in limited cases, can disable genes carrying undesirable traits and replace them with genes carrying desirable traits. While these sorts of developments pose many possibilities for altering various organisms and eradicating certain diseases and disabilities, gene therapy remains experimental.

For obvious reasons, certain groups, such as the National Multiple Sclerosis Society and the Cystic Fibrosis Foundation, support genetic engineering in the hopes of dramatic cures being developed. Still others, like certain religious groups, oppose genetic engineering.

Environmentalism and Social Change

The vast majority of Americans consider themselves "environmentally friendly." Furthermore, estimates show that some 14 million people in the United States belong to one or more of the 150 nationwide environmental organizations. A few of the best-known of these organizations are Greenpeace, the Sierra Club, and the Natural Resources Defense Council.

Contemporary environmentalism has moved in several directions. Many local grassroots environmental groups have emerged to deal with alleged environmental hazards. And many large and influential environmental groups have become increasingly visible politically by lobbying for causes such as energy conservation, elimination of air and water pollution as well as safety and environmental hazards, and the protection of wildlife and natural resources. Both grassroots and large, influential organizations generally work for social change within the bounds of the law via education, electoral politics, lobbying, and lawsuits. Some smaller, more radical groups, however, may resort to illegal methods, such as threats and sabotage.

Sociologists have concerned themselves with what they call **environmental racism**. The U.S. Environmental Protection Agency has indicated that ethnic and racial minorities are disproportionately exposed to lead, dangerous chemicals, dust, carbon monoxide, ozone, sulfur, sulfur dioxide, and the emissions from hazardous waste sites. Activists within Hispanic-, African-, Asian-, and Native-American communities explain environmental racism in light of their poor neighborhoods that may sit close to industrial sites and dumping grounds. Such exposure leads minorities to suffer disproportionate rates of cancer, birth defects, and chemical poisoning. Awareness of the impact of such exposure has led many minority communities to mobilize their resources to eliminate environmental hazards.

The environmental movement, like other social movements, has encountered resistance. In fact, this resistance has grown into its own social movement. Founded in the late 1980s, the **wise-use movement** calls for balance in society's need for clean air, drinkable water, and undisturbed wilderness areas with the equally important need for food, jobs, energy, and tourist sites. Proponents of wise-use often take an anti-environmental approach, decrying what they believe constitutes "nature worship" on the part of environmentalists. For instance, they do not oppose opening public lands to mining, logging, grazing, and energy development. They may also allow dumping of hazardous wastes into rivers, cutting down forests, and developing businesses in national parks. The wise-use movement has traditionally received political and financial support from such groups as the American Farm Bureau Federation and the National Cattlemen's Association.

Resisting Social Change

Some people resist social change. In the midst of continual techno-logical breakthroughs, some people harbor **vested interests** (finan-cial or otherwise) in maintaining the status quo. These people lose something in response to social change. For example, the American Psychiatric Association (APA) has lobbied incessantly to prevent clinical psychologists from gaining prescription privileges. Other people may feel insecure about trying to adapt to an ever-changing society.

Economic factors take a hand in resisting social change. Conflict theorists complain that capitalistic systems encourage owners to pro-tect their assets at the expense of workers. Protecting their assets may mean ignoring safety standards or putting pressure on government officials to lessen state regulations.

Cultural factors also play a central role in resistance to social change. When technology enters a society, non-material culture must respond to changes in material culture. **Culture lag** refers to the time during which previous aspects of a society still need to "catch up" to cultural advances. For example, certain religious groups, such as the Roman Catholic Church, promote large families and regard contra-ceptive methods that limit family size as immoral. In other words, a lag exists between aspects of non-material culture (religious beliefs) and material culture (reproductive technologies).

Social movements typically question a culture's established state of affairs. In the United States today, both the gay rights and feminist movements challenge society's definitions of "natural order"—that heterosexuality is the only sexual standard and that females should submit to males. Resistance to such social movements remains pre-dictably strong.

Notes

Notes

Notes

Notes

Notes

Notes